THE STUFFED OWL RETURNS

Praise for
THE STUFFED OWL RETURNS

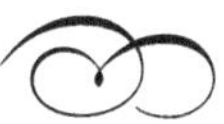

"And not a moment too soon."

~ *Clockwatchers' Annual*

"Belongs in every bathroom."

~ *Procrastination Today*

"This slim volume ..."

~ Tusenelda Worth, author of *Iambic and So Are You*

"For word noodlers everywhere."

~ *Poets' Education Society*

"If I had known my feeblest works would be retained in the world's memory, I would have been busier at the fireplace."

~ Ichabod Weltschmerz, author of *Mesmerizations*

"I don't understand why the narrator doesn't like these."

~ Darby Nash, age 7

THE STUFFED OWL RETURNS

Newly Collected Poetical Mishaps and Absurdities

Edited with introduction and commentary by

Lindsay Crane

Print and Pixel Books

ISBN (softcover): 978-1-7369864-1-7
ISBN (ebook): 978-1-7369864-2-4
Library of Congress Control Number: 2021907938

Published by Print and Pixel Books, Lafayette, California

Cover photo by Lindsay Crane
Owl courtesy of Lindsay Wildlife Experience, Walnut Creek, California, a natural history museum, wildlife hospital and educational institution, lindsaywildlife.org

Book Design by Sun Editing & Book Design, suneditwrite.com

Interior Photos:
"Drum," National Library of Russia, Unsplash.com
"Bee," Myriams-Fotos, Pixabay.com
"Child praying," Dimitris Vetsikas, Pixabay.com
"Snail," Alexas_Fotos, Unsplash.com
"Sea rock ocean," Creative Commons (no name attributed)
"Castle in mist," Tim Rebkavets, Unsplash.com
"Ship on fire," Noupload, Pixabay.com
"Cleopatra," Pixabay.com (no name attributed)
"Victorian lovers," Hulton archive (no name attributed)
"Flying cow," Urs Flueeler/Epa-Efe Shutterstock.com

Preface

A garden is a lovesome thing, God wot!

DID YOU EVER WONDER where this gem came from? It was commemorated in the 1930 classic ***The Stuffed Owl: An Anthology of Bad Verse.*** We might never have learned of this poet, one Thomas Edward Brown (1830–1897), had the editors not rescued him from the obscurity into which he had fallen.

A surprising number of scholars and writers who were famous in their own day likewise fell from eminence and are represented in this book. More surprisingly, even the greatest poets whose names were *not* writ on water have produced yards of rubbish. The lesson seems to be this: Write down everything that crosses your mind and one percent of it may have poetic significance. Examples of this technique are to be found throughout this slim volume.

This is very encouraging for us wannabe poets.

It may be bad for our spiritual development, but it's so much fun to giggle at bad poetry. Using a familiar self-absolving phrase, let us designate it a Guilty Pleasure. Readers of this book are encouraged to indulge their voyeuristic journey into kitsch, while cloaking it in the disinterested love of good poetry and sympathizing with the muse outraged.

Contents

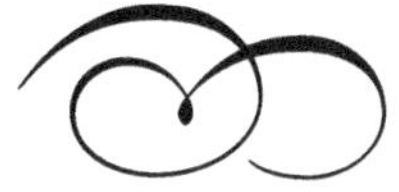

Preface vii

To Be Read in a Bookshop While Deciding Whether to Purchase This Tome . . . xi

Introduction 1

How to Stuff an Owl 9

Poets and Pratfalls 15

Intermission 83

The Compleat Mischief 101

Parting Shots 123

Bonus Elements in the Original *Stuffed Owl* 125

Subject Index 129

Author Index 135

About the Editor 139

To Be Read in a Bookshop

While Deciding Whether to Purchase This Tome

Whither have I been drawn
By the dead weight of my posterior?

~ Edmond Rostand, *Cyrano de Bergerac*, Act III

Daffodil bulbs instead of balls
Stared from the sockets of his eyes!

~ T.S. Eliot, *Whispers of Immortality*

I salute you both with the spirit of copulation.

~ Cyril Tourneur, *The Atheist's Tragedy*, Act I, Scene 2

I cannot tell who loves the skeleton of a poor marmoset.

~ Richard Lovelace, *La Bella Bona-Roba*

Shapcot! To thee the fairy state
I with discretion dedicate.

~ Robert Herrick, *Oberon's Feast*

Why has not Man a microscopic eye?
For this plain reason, Man is not a fly.

~ Alexander Pope, *Essay on Man, I* (VI)

The aged minstrel stood aghast
So hastily Fitz-James shot past.

~ Sir Walter Scott, *Lady of the Lake*

I am wound up in deep astonishment!

~ John Keats, *Otho the Great,*
Act I, Scene 1

Did you fear some scrofula out of the
unflagging pregnancy?

~ Walt Whitman, *Song of Myself*

But thus in oak's true shade recounted he,
Which now in night's deep shade sheep
heard of me.

~ Sir Philip Sidney, *Shepherd Song,*
Poems from Arcadia

Such fragments might kindly be considered unwitting experiments in the haiku form. Or perhaps they are evidence that artists are not always the best judges of their own work. For example, Shakespeare, who carefully published several long poems (unreadable today), died without having made provision for the publication of his much superior plays. Two of his fellow actors, Heminges and Condell, spent seven years collecting tattered or pirated copies, correcting them, and publishing the First Folio in 1623. In their introduction to that majestic tome, they conclude their labors with an address to readers that I echo for this modest one:

> Well ! It is now publique, & you wil stand
> for your priviledges wee know: to read,
> and censure. Do so, but buy it first.

Introduction

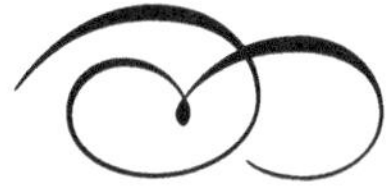

Bad verse, too, has its canons. My distinguished predecessors, D.B. Wyndham Lewis and Charles Lee, state that bad verse is characterized by bathos (the sudden slide from the sublime to the ridiculous), poverty of imagination, sentimentality, pomposity, and banality. They were careful, however, to distinguish Bad Bad verse from Good Bad verse, describing the former as "vast, and confusing in its tropical luxuriance," and offered mostly by amateurs. By contrast, "Bad verse of the good kind is innocent of faults of craftsmanship ... [and] has an eerie, supernal beauty."

Wyndham Lewis and Lee, naming their collection after a baffling line in Wordsworth, justly published primarily *Good* Bad Poetry. The startling metaphor, the ill-chosen word, and the uprush of soggy sentiment give us the joyous shudder that mere doggerel cannot. The present editor offers two examples of bad verse and invites the reader to distinguish the good from the bad.

It is four and forty years ago
Since the one of us the other did ken;
And we have had, betwixt us two,
Of children either nine or ten.

~ Anonymous, 16th century

As I sit writing here, sick and grown old,
Not my least burden is that dulness of the years, querilities,
Ungracious glooms, aches, lethargy, constipation, whimpering ennui,
May filter in my daily songs.

~ Whitman, *As I Sit Writing Here*

Bad verse is not parody, but sincere and serious. Eminent poets with straight faces have issued the following:

I must die like a sick eagle looking at the sky.

~ Keats, *On Seeing the Elgin Marbles*

I submit me! Of vanities under the sun,
Pride seized me at last as concupiscence first,
Crapulosity ever.

~ Browning, *Fust and His Friends*

Rhyme and rhythm can enhance a poetic work, but "Rules for Rules' Sake" can also produce absurdities like this:

Tumpty-tum-tump; Tumpty-tum-tump—
Hark to the sound of the drums,
Tumpty-tum-tump; Tumpty-tum-tump—
The beat and the thud that you feel in your blood
The heart-shaking rhythm that comes
With thunder and throb of the drums.
The drums! The drums!

~ Berton Braley, *The Drums*

Braley lived from 1882 to 1966. I had never heard of him either, but during his lifetime he published in many magazines and had one lyric set to music by John Philip Sousa. He also edited *The World's One Thousand Best Poems* in ten volumes, commemorating his own (very dated) tastes.

Looking into an allied art form, we may be grateful that the judges of the Prix de Rome looked past their competition's rules and admonished young composer Georges Bizet so gently:

> This work is distinguished by its ease and brilliance, its bold and youthful style, qualities precious for the comic genre for which the composer shows a marked inclination. We are obliged, however, to censure M. Bizet for having written an *opera buffa* when the regulations demanded a mass.

Missteps Great and Small

I have added representatives of the noble art of poetic pratfall in both historical directions, beginning in the period before my esteemed predecessors opened their anthology, and carrying on after they discreetly closed the curtain on the modern age. The original editors deprived themselves of many a delicious *frisson* of aesthetic horror—a sort of literary Miss Manners sniff—by excluding the Cavalier poets (e.g., Carew, Suckling, Herrick). The Cavaliers' accusatory sulks of self-pity uttered when rejected by maidens who had not invited their advances—the "Woe R Us" mentality—fertilized a rich vein of languishing affectation.

Shakespeare and Sidney, despite their stature, really must be included. Hard as it is to believe, the author of Sonnet 73 *(That time of year thou may'st in me behold)* was also capable of this resistible solicitation from Venus to Adonis:

Here come and sit where never serpent hisses,
And being set, I'll smother thee with kisses.

And the courtier, soldier, and diplomat who penned *Thou Blind Man's Mark* could also produce lines as clumsy as "Why shouldst thou toil our thorny soil to till?" Simple honesty compels us to admit them to the poets' hall of shame—but serves also to remind us that genius, too, has its boots in fertilizer. Bach stood on the shoulders of a hundred tunemakers; sculptors Michelangelo and Bernini sprang from the culture that erected a thousand terra cotta roadside shrines.

The dross rate of great poets is rarely considered. Keats and Browning produced prodigious amounts of twaddle, but Whitman's ratio is surely equal to theirs. The voice that is capable of the deep and sonorous cadences of *O Captain, My Captain* and *A Sight in Camp* could apparently with equal pleasure produce, preserve, and publish such slight musings as this, from *Song of Myself:* "I keep as delicate around the bowels as around the head and heart."

An Embarrassment of Riches

Some iconoclastic eras in the arts exist for the purpose of overthrowing existing conventions, to make fresh the canvas, to cleanse the aesthetic palate. Then those who follow can see and hear afresh. This is a legitimate function. I see much of modern art in this light—performing a kind of janitorial service which must be applauded alike by the judicious, the just, and the relieved.

However, this doesn't mean we must admire junk. Bits of cardboard, yarn, and metal scattered over a museum room gain the sobriquet "installation" and the respectful attention of critics, who develop new vocabularies to show that they are *au courant*. It is hard to know who is using whom. In the literary world, modern utterances are so often mere sonorous honkings of the klaxon, coupled with an inability to recognize the grotesque, as we see in the examples in this compendium by Jarrell and Hugo. Even a basic sense of manners is lacking. Do we really want to know that the art of poetry reminds some versifier of a brassiere?

Modern aesthetic also gives dangerous approval to the idea that declaring one's emotions is, *ipso facto,* valuable. In psychotherapeutic terms, of course, this is so: as a former practitioner of that elusive profession, I grant myself the right to make this pronouncement. But however significant they may be on the lived human level, emotional expressions are not, of themselves, art.

With such an embarrassment of modern riches, the attentive reader may ask, "Where are the modern poets? This collection shortchanges the great word noodlers of the 20th and 21st centuries!"

Answer: Mounds of material by modern poets could not be included because: I didn't know about them.

How to Stuff an Owl

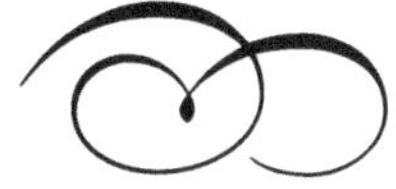

Once you have read (and reread) this collection, you may ask yourself, "Where can I find *more* poetic blunders?" It's easy to find bad *old* poems – just fetch Collected Works of any versifier, especially the early pages where juvenilia are to be found, and plod along until you find them. Or try the art of letting the book fall open and pointing with your eyes closed.

To find more *modern* bad poetry,

- Look in any issue of the *New Yorker,* or
- Create your own. Here are methods the poets of the past have used to incite their muses to perform the unspeakable.

Titillating Titles

No one will ever equal the titling brilliance of Ogden Nash, whose poems include *Oh, Stop Apologizing All Over the Place* and *You Cad, Why Don't You Cringe?* and *Don't Worry, Darling, It's Blood All Right.* But we can savor the tone-deafness that gave us:

- *The Ballad of Bouillabaisse* (extracted later in this anthology)
- *Strictly Germ-Proof*
- *Kafoozalum*

Nostalgia Myalgia

To indulge in sweetly painful yearning for its own sake; a non-fattening addiction.

> Ah happy hills! ah pleasing shade!
> Ah fields beloved in vain!
> Where once my careless childhood stray'd
> A stranger yet to pain!
>
> ~ Thomas Gray, from *Ode on a Distant Prospect of Eton College*

Awful Rhymes and Rhythms

"Doggerel" is the less polite term for rocking-horse meter and strained rhymes, when the versifier obeys the rules too obsequiously.

Charlotte was a married lady,
  and a moral man was Werther,
and for all the wealth of Indies,
  would do nothing for to hurt her.

So he sighed and pined and ogled,
  and his passion boiled and bubbled
Till he blew his silly brains out
  And no more was by it troubled.

~ William M. Thackeray,
from *Sorrows of Werther*

Bathos and the Sudden Turn

Even our language's greatest dramatic poet could slip on a banana peel.

Good lords, conduct him to his regiment;
I'll strive, with troubled thoughts, to take a nap.

~ Shakespeare, *Richard II,* Act V, Scene 3

Audacity

Pope was nothing if not audacious. His extended poem, *Essay on Man, Epistle I,* is titled:

Of the Nature and State of Man, with Respect to the Universe.

Apostrophize the Improbable

To the determined poet, there is nothing that cannot be addressed directly. Anne Finch, Countess of Winchelsea (1661–1720), moved in high society until Charles II was exiled, but returned to luxury and vigorously defended women's literary skill. Her verse was appreciated by Wordsworth and Woolf.

What art thou, Spleen, which ev'ry thing dost ape?

~ Anne Finch, Countess of Winchelsea, *The Spleen*

Yes, I Majored in Classics

Extra credit if you know who the heck these people are.

Epeirus high was honest Klaius' nest,
To Strephon Aeole's land first breathing lent,
But East and West were join'd by friendship's hest.
As Strephon's ear and heart to Klaius bent,
So Klaius' soul did in his Strephon rest:
Still both their flocks flocking together went,
As if they would of owners' humour be;
As eke their pipes did well as friends agree.

~ Philip Sidney, *Poems from Arcadia*

Neologisms

When one's thesaurus is lost or in the other room—invent!

> In every place the ugsome sights I saw.
>
> ~ Henry Howard, *Virgil's Aeneid* (translation)

> Out of the hitherwhere into the yon—
> Stay the hopes we are leaning on.
>
> ~ James Whitcomb Riley, *Out of the Hitherwhere*

We Were Hoping Not to Think of That

Pope's ridicule of other writers, while making enemies in his day, achieves the status of Bad Bad Verse:

> How hints, like spawn, scarce quick in embryo lie,
> How new-born nonsense first is taught to cry;
> Maggots half-formed in rhyme exactly meet,
> And learn to crawl upon poetic feet.
>
> ~ from *The Dunciad*

Poets and Pratfalls

Thomas Wyatt (1503–1542)

The *fons et origo* of English poetry, Wyatt introduced the sonnet into our language but also became entangled in the turbulent, bloody Tudor politics of his age and was twice imprisoned and released, before dying at age 39. He also sired a son who was beheaded after leading Wyatt's Rebellion, fortunately after our poet's death.

> In spite of hap, hap hath well hapt.
>
> ~ *In Faith, I Wot Not What to Say*

Henry Howard (1517–1547)

Like many noblemen of that century, Howard learned to write verse and is credited with devising the English form of the sonnet. Like Wyatt, he couldn't resist hazarding the bloody court politics of Henry VIII and was beheaded as a result. He was ahead of his time in using blank verse, shown here in his translation of Virgil.

He with his hands strave to unloose the knots
Whose sacred fillets all besprinkled were
With filth of gory blood and venom rank,
And to the stars such dreadful shouts he sent,
Like to the sound the roaring bull forth lows
Which from the altar wounded doth astart,
The swerving axe when he shakes from his neck.
The serpents twain, with hasted trail they glide
To Pallas' temple, and her towers of height:
Under the feet of the which goddess stern,
Hidden behind her target's boss they crept.
New gripes of dread then pierce our trembling breasts.
...
With senseless bodies every street is spread,
Each palace, and sacred porch of the gods.
Nor yet alone the Troyan blood was shed.
Manhood ofttimes into the vanquisht breast
Returns, whereby some victor Greeks are slain.
Cruel complaints and terror everywhere,
And plenty of grisly pictures of death.

~ *Virgil's Aeneid* (translation)

Fulke Greville (1554–1628)

Greville had more names than the hero of a Russian novel. Close friend and admirer of Sidney, he was 1st Baron Brooke, de jure 13th Baron Latimer, and 5th Baron Willoughby de Broke KB, PC.

There was a time before the times of Story
When Nature reign'd instead of Laws or Arts,
And mortal gods, with men made up the glory
Of one Republic by united hearts.
  Earth was the common seat, their conversation
  In saving love, and ours in adoration.

~ First verse (of 664) in *A Treatise of Monarchy*

Besides, chaste life years easilier* may observe,
Which temper in cathedral-dignity,
Though wives be lawful, yet doth well deserve,
As to their functions leaving them more free;
  Instance their learned works that liv'd alone,
  Where married bishops left us few, or none.

~ Verse 228 in *A Treatise of Monarchy*

What make these many laws, these reins of Pow'r
Wherewith mankind thus fetter'd is and bound;
These divers worships, which men's souls deflow'r;
Nature and God, with novelty confound?
  'Tis ignorance, Sin, Infidelity
  By which we fall'n from our creation be.

~ First verse (of 114) in *A Treatise of Religion*

* *"easilier"? – Ed.*

Sir Philip Sidney (1554–1586)

Though we lament the early death of Sidney in his century's version of the grim reaping of young poets (viz. Wyatt, Suckling, and Marlowe), we should take comfort for one reason: he was poised to stifle Shakespeare's dramatic muse. In an otherwise excellent essay (*Apology for Poesy*), he defended the classical unities of time, place, and action, which Shakespeare defied with cheerful abandon. Sidney's early death after the battle at Zutphen cleared the way for Hamlet, Falstaff, and Beatrice.

Oh, heavenly fool, thy most kiss-worthy face
Anger invests with such a lovely grace
That anger's self I needs must kiss again.

~ *Astrophel and Stella*, 73

O honey'd sighs! which from the breast do rise,
Whose pants do make unspilling cream to flow,
Wing'd with whose breath, so pleasing zephyrs blow,
As might refresh the hell where my soul fries.

~ *Astrophel and Stella*, 100

In faith, good Histor, long is your delay
From holy marriage, sweet and surest mean,
Our foolish lust in honest rule to stay.
I pray thee do to Lalus' sample lean:

Thou seest how frisk and jolly now he is,
That last day seem'd he could not chew a bean.
Who for each fickle fear from virtue shrinks
Shall in this life embrace no worthy thing;
No mortal man the cup of surety drink;
The heavens do not good haps in handfuls bring.

~ *Geron and Histor*

O words which fall like summer dew on me,
O breath more sweet than is the growing bean,
O tongue in which all honey'd liquors be,
O voice that doth the thrush in shrillness stain:
Do you say still, this is her promise due,
That she is mine as I to her am true.

Gay hair, more gay than straw when harvest lies,
Lips red and plump as cherry's ruddy side,
Eyes fair and great like fair great ox's eyes,
O breast in which two white sheep swell in pride:

Join you with me, to seal this promise due,
That she be mine as I to her am true.
But thou white skin, as white as curds well prest,
As smooth as sleekstone like it smooths each part,
And thou dear flesh, as soft as wool new drest,
And yet as hard as brawn made hard by art:
First four but say, next four their saying seal,
But you must pay the gage of promis'd weal.

~ *Arcadian Duologue*

Thomas Lodge (1558–1625)

Abandoning his legal training to turn to literature, Lodge produced plays, essays, translations, and a story that was used by Shakespeare for *As You Like It.* Late in life he became a physician, practiced medicine, and published medical works. His grasp of apian anatomy here seems dubious.

Love in my bosom like a bee
Doth suck his sweet:
Now with his wings he plays with me,
Now with his feet.

~ *Rosalind's Madrigal*

Mary Sidney, Countess of Pembroke (1561–1621)

Niece of Queen Elizabeth's favorite Leicester, sister of Sir Philip Sidney, she was one of the earliest Englishwomen to be an acclaimed author. A scholar of that time mentioned her in the same breath as Shakespeare—deservedly, if the rumor has merit that she wrote some of his sonnets. Marrying into the nobility, she held a salon frequented by Spenser, Samuel Daniel, Drayton, and Jonson, and of whom it was written, "She was the greatest patroness of wit and learning of any lady in her time."

Woods, hills, and rivers now are desolate,
Sith* he is gone the which them all did grace:
And all the fields do wail their widow state,
Sith death their fairest flow'r did late deface.
  The fairest flow'r in field that ever grew,
  Was Astrophel; that was, we all may rue.

What cruel hand of cursed foe unknown,
Hath cropped the stalk which bore so fair a flow'r?
Untimely cropped, before it well were grown,
And clean defaced in untimely hour.
  Great loss to all that ever him did see,
  Great loss to all, but greatest loss to me.

~ *The Doleful Lay of Clorinda*

* *sith = since*

Michael Drayton (1563–1631)

One year older than Shakespeare, and born like him in Warwickshire, Drayton was also drawn to composing dramas based on English history. However, it is safe to say that the younger playwright did not publish 18 volumes in verse describing the topographical and antiquarian highlights of England and Wales. Drayton's sonnets are among the pinnacles of English literature, but he also composed a satire, *The Man in the Moon,* and another one called *The Owl.*

Ye scaly creatures, gaze upon her eye,
And never after with your kind make war;
O steal the accents from her lips that fly,
Which like the tunes of the Celestials are,
And them to your sick amorous thoughts apply,
Compared with which, Arion's* did but jar;
Wrap them in air, and when black tempests rage,
Use them as charms the rough seas to assuage.

~ *The Barons' Wars,* III, 48

* *Arion = mythical horse god*

William Shakespeare (1564–1616)

We must be grateful that theatres were reopened in 1598, or else Shakespeare might have perpetrated more closet musings along the lines of *Venus and Adonis* (which inexplicably was his most popular published work in his lifetime) or *The Phoenix and the Turtle.* Clearly, character, situation, and action stimulated his highest portrayals, rhapsodies, and turn of wit. Yet there are a few regrettable lines in the plays. *Hamlet,* dear Hamlet, has a few groaners. Claudius prods his wife to explain why she's sighing loudly in despair. "There's matter in these sighs, these profound heaves," he intones. Fortunately, the following is only "attributed."

The sun look't on the world with glorious eye,
Yet not so wistly as this queen on him.
He, spying her, bounced in, whereas he stood:
"O Jove," quoth she, "Why was not I a flood?"

~ attributed to Shakespeare,
The Passionate Pilgrim, No. 6.

Late in his career, Shakespeare began to collaborate with other playwrights, launching a cottage industry of scholars debating which lines are his.

Scoffing at scholars who think otherwise, I blame the following on Fletcher.

When her arms,
Able to lock Jove from a synod, shall
By warranting moonlight corslet thee, O when
Her twining cherries shall their sweetness fall
Upon thy tasteful lips, what wilt thou think
Of rotten kings or blubbered queens, what care
For what thou feel'st not, what thou feel'st being able
To make Mars spurn his drum?
…

Dear Palamon, dearer in love than blood
And our prime cousin, yet unhardened in
The crimes of nature, let us leave the city
Thebes, and the temptings in't, before we further
Sully our gloss of youth;
And here to keep in abstinence we shame
As in incontinence; for not to swim
In the aid of the current were almost to sink,
At least to frustrate striving; and to follow
The common stream, 'twould bring us to an eddy
Where we should turn or drown; if labor through
Our gain but life and weakness.

~ Shakespeare and John Fletcher,
The Two Noble Kinsmen,
Act I, Scenes 1 and 2

Christopher Marlowe (1564–1593)

Whether he died in a brawl or overseas in a witness protection program, Marlowe was the celebrated precursor of Shakespeare, both in verse and drama. In the first selection, a disloyal courtier is asked to describe a foe. The listener proclaims that he has understood it, which is more than we can do.

Of stature tall, and straightly fashioned
Like his desire, lift upwards and divine.
So large of limbs, his joints so strongly knit,
Such breadth of shoulders as might mainly bear
Old Atlas's burden. 'Twixt his manly pitch,
A pearl more worth than all the world is plac'd,
Wherein by curious sovereignty of art
Are fix'd his piercing instruments of sight,
Whose fiery circles bear encompassed
A heaven of heavenly bodies in their spheres,
That guides his steps and actions to the throne
Where honour sits invested royally.

~ *Tamburlaine,* Part I, Act 2, Scene 1

Chaste Hero to herself thus softly said:
Were I the saint he worships, I would hear him;
And as she spake these words, came somewhat near him.
...

Then treasure is abused,
When misers keep it; being put to loan,
In time it will return us two for one.

~ *Hero and Leander*

John Donne (1572–1631)

The naive trust in metaphor as a basis for cosmological speculation permits the segues that lead from a flea to the sublime, or the Pythagorean theorem to the nature of love. Donne is the great practitioner of this metaphysic, an enjoyable reconciliation between what passed for science in their age and what was really art—the reverse of our own day.

For if the sinewy thread my brain lets fall through
every part
Can tie those parts and make me one of all
These hairs, which upward grow, and strength
and art have from a better brain,
Can better do't.

~ *The Funeral*

Robert Herrick (1591–1674)

Herrick urged others to gather rosebuds while they may, but seems not to have done so himself. Here we can admire his religious side.

Here a little child I stand
Heaving up my either hand;
Cold as paddocks* though they be,
Here I lift them up to Thee
For a benison to fall
On our meat and on us all. Amen

~ *A Child's Grace*

* *paddock = fish*

Henry King (1592–1669)

Yet another poet who served his religion, in his case as Bishop of Chichester and Dean of Rochester; hence the epithet for his wife.

> Accept, thou shrine of my dead saint,
> Instead of dirges, this complaint:
> And for sweet flowers to crown thy hearse
> Receive a strew of weeping verse.
>
> ~ *The Exequy*

Thomas Carew (1595–1640)

Friend of Jonson and Suckling, admirer of Donne, frank celebrator of the erotic, Carew composed lyrics, songs, pastorals, poetic dialogues, and elegies. Celia was the subject of many of his verses.

That lovely spot which thou dost see
In Celia's bosom was a bee.
Who built her amorous spicy rest
In the Hyblas of either breast ...
There feasting on ambrosial meat
A rolling file of balmy sweat
(as in soft murmurs before death
Swan-like she sung) choked up her breath

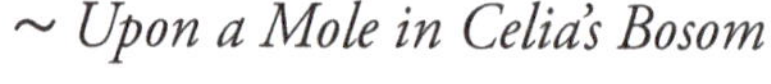
~ *Upon a Mole in Celia's Bosom*

Madam, men say you keep with dropping eyes
Your sorrows fresh, watering the rose that lies
Fall'n from your cheeks upon your dear lord's hearse.
Alas! those odours now no more can pierce
His cold pale nostril, nor the crimson dye
Present a graceful blush to his dark eye.
Think you that flood of pearly moisture hath
The virtue fabled of old Aeson's bath?

~ *To the Countess of Anglesey*

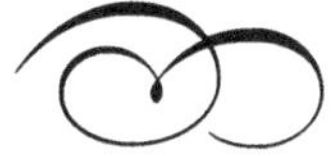

SIR JOHN SUCKLING (1609–*after* 1641)

Perhaps the only poet to have invented a card game (cribbage), Suckling spent whole mornings in bed practicing, so he could take unfair advantage of the gentry with whom he played. He allegedly used marked cards and, according to antiquarian John Aubrey, won £20,000. Suckling paid to stage his play, *Aglaura,* which is festooned with macabre exchanges.

Jacqueline. You will not, I pray,
    Breathe one fragmented letter of this tale.
Jacques. Drowned lips are not more certain.
Jacqueline. The frailty of our sexes!
Jacques. It must come out, like pus; our nature's so.
...

Aglaura. We must not be seen, otherwise I weep.
Thomas. The stars will weep all night long, mightily
    Bound to their canopies, because they cannot do
    what we do.
Aglaura. You warm me well.*
Thomas. Like death I come, while grooms and
        courtly ants
    Inside their chambers fart and snore. A kiss!

* *Wait till she hears his next appeal. – Ed.*

Loath to abandon his last line's earthy metaphor, Suckling later proclaimed:

> Love is the fart
> Of every heart;
> It pains a man when 'tis kept close,
> And others doth offend when 'tis let loose.
>
> ~ *If, When Don Cupid's Dart*

Richard Crashaw (1613–1649)

The reader of the sole example of Crashaw's works in the present compilation will not be surprised to learn that he was profoundly religious, converted from the Anglican to the Catholic church, fled England when Puritans came to power, and wrote verses about saints, martyrs, and Jesus.

Suppose He had been tabled at thy teats,
Thy hunger feel not what He eats;
He'll have his teat ere long (a bloody one)
The mother then must suck the son.

~ *Luke 11.*

Richard Lovelace (1617–1657)

Prison (a destination surprisingly common to our poets) stimulated this bold man to his greatest heights ("Stone walls do not a prison make"). Unjustly neglected are his later works *The Grasse-hopper, The Snayl, The Falcon,* and *The Toad and Spyder.*

Depose your finger of that ring,
        And crowne mine with't awhile;
Now I restor't. Pray, does it bring
        Back with it more of soile?
Or shines it not as innocent,
As honest, as before 'twas lent?

~ *Sonnet*

Compendious Snayl! thou seem'st to me
Large Euclid's strict epitome;
And in each diagram dost fling
Thee from the point unto the ring.
A figure now triangulare,
An oval now, and now a square,
And then a serpentine, dost crawl,
Now a straight line, now crook'd, now all.
...

Thou, thine own daughter, then, and sire,
That son and mother art intire,
That big still with thy self dost go,
And liv'st an aged embrio;
That like the cubbs of India,
Thou from thy self a while dost play;
But frighted with a dog or gun,
In thine own belly thou dost run,
And as thy house was thine own womb,
So thine own womb concludes thy tomb.

~ *The Snayl*

Upon a day, when the Dog-star
Unto the world proclaim'd a war,
And poyson bark'd from black throat,
And from his jaws infection shot,
Under a deadly hen-bane shade
With slime infernal mists are made,
Met the two dreaded enemies,
Having their weapons in their eyes.
...
First from his den rolls forth that load
Of spite and hate, the speckl'd toad,
And from his chaps a foam doth spawn,
Such as the loathed three heads yawn;
Defies his foe with a fell spit,
To wade through death to meet with it;
Then in his self the lymbeck turns,*
And his elixir'd poyson urns.

~ *The Toad and Spyder, A Duell*

* *limbeck = device for distilling*

Andrew Marvell (1621–1678)

Luckily for us, Marvell abandoned his college practice of writing verse in Latin and Greek. Luckily for Milton, Marvell retained enough prestige even after flirting with the anti-royalists that he was able to prevent the restored monarchy from executing that great scalawag.

> Vaster than empires, and more slow,
> My vegetable love shall grow.
>
> ~ *To His Coy Mistress*

John Dryden (1631–1700)

The trouble with being the poet laureate is that one must produce works that praise the royal family, their doings, and national events. The first to have this honor, Dryden also indulged in translations and drama.

Thou sing with him, thou booby? – Never pipe
Was so profan'd to touch that blubber'd lip.
Dunce at the best! in streets but scarce allow'd
To tickle, on thy straw, the stupid crowd.
...
Ye boys, who pluck the flow'rs and spoil the spring,
Beware the secret snake that shoots a sting.

~ Dryden's translation of Virgil's *Pastoral III*

Half-wits are fleas; so little and so light,
We scarce could know they live, but that they bite.

~ Prologue to the play *All for Love*

ALEXANDER POPE (1688–1744)

The undisputed master of the heroic couplet, Pope satirized love, society, epics, and other poets. His translations of Homer earned him fame and funds; his editions of Shakespeare less so, since he took it upon himself to delete or change passages he didn't like. (In the following century, censoring sexy and irreverent passages to create "The Family Shakespeare" earned Thomas Bowdler a verb in the English language). Pope rarely made ridiculous errors; below you may read one unintentional lapse and one created on purpose.

For know, Sir Knight, of gentle blood I came;
I loathe a whore, and startle at the name.

~ *January and May*

The snappish cur (the passengers' annoy)
Close at my heel with yelping treble flies;
The whimpering girl, and hoarser-screaming boy
Join to the yelping treble, shrilling cries;
The scolding quean* to louder notes doth rise,
To her full pipes the grunting hog replies;
The grunting hogs alarm the neighbors round,
And curs, girls, boys, and scolds, in the deep bass
are drown'd.

~ Imitations of English Poets Done by the Author in his Youth, after Spenser, *The Alley.*

* *quean = impudent woman*

Thomas Gray (1716–1771)

So uncertain of his artistry that he published only thirteen poems in his lifetime, Gray was nevertheless offered the post of Poet Laureate, but he declined the honor. Perhaps he was preoccupied by his academic duties as professor at Cambridge. We may rejoice in this contribution to our collective wisdom: "Where ignorance is bliss, 'tis folly to be wise."

Ambition this shall tempt to rise,
   Then whirl the wretch from high
To bitter Scorn a sacrifice
   And grinning Infamy.
The stings of Falsehood those shall try,
And hard Unkindness' alter'd eye,
   That mocks the tear it forced to flow;
And keen Remorse with blood defil'd,
And moody Madness laughing wild
   Amid severest woe.

~ *Ode on a Distant Prospect of Eton College*

William Collins (1721–1759)

Living in London on an allowance from his cousin while striving for a literary career, Collins received uneven evaluations during his lifetime and after. Even being noticed sufficiently to be disparaged by Johnson, Gray, and Dickens is something of an achievement.

How sleep the brave, who sink to rest,
By all their country's wishes blest!
When Spring, with dewy fingers cold
Returns to deck their hallow'd mould,
She there shall dress a sweeter sod
Than Fancy's feet have ever trod.
...

By fairy hands their knell is rung;
By forms unseen their dirge is sung;
There Honour comes, a pilgrim grey,
To bless the turf that wraps their clay;
And Freedom shall awhile repair
To dwell, a weeping hermit, there!

~*How Sleep the Brave*

James Boswell (1740–1795)

Johnson's loyal lapdog and biographer also committed some of his sentiments to verse, including one bravely entitled *The Turnspittiad.* Known among his friends for dreaming up whimsical projects, he admitted, "There have been many people who built castles in the air, but I believe I am the first that ever attempted to live in them." Alas, Boswell was pro-slavery and composed a long poem to say so. Rarely has the classical art been so disgraced by its practitioners. So it is with no remorse that we may disdain the following samples of his verse.

Lord Lofty on a sick bed lies;
His Lady, much afflicted, cries.
Think you 'tis for her husband's sake?
If so, you're in a flat mistake.
She mourns a different matter far—
Her pug has broke a china jar.

~*On a Marriage between a Beautiful Young Lady and a Coarse Hulk of a Gentleman.*

Delightful pastime of my tender age,
While yet I view'd life's title-page,
And with the gilded letters please,
Sweetly blew and softly sneez'd.

~*Ode on Whistling*

Ann Radcliffe (1764–1823)

This shy, retiring lady practically invented the Gothic novel, with gruesome deaths, skeletal relics, and frightful abbeys with caged starved prisoners, initiating a taste for delicious horrors that continues to this day. Naturally, she was a huge success. Satirizing this theme in *Northanger Abbey,* Jane Austen has her naïve heroine longing to read the latest thrillers: *The Castle of Wolfenbach, Necromancer of the Black Forest, Orphan of the Rhine,* and *Horrid Mysteries.* "Are they all horrid?" she eagerly asks her friend. "Are you *sure* they are all horrid?" Luckily for us, Radcliffe also composed poems, which were included in her grotesque tales.

High mid Alverna's awful steeps,
   Eternal shades, and silence dwell,
Save, when the gale resounding sweeps,
   Sad strains are faintly heard to swell:

Enthron'd amid the wild impending rocks,
Involv'd in clouds, and brooding future woe,
The demon Superstition Nature shocks,
And waves her Sceptre o'er the world below.

Around her throne, amid the mingling glooms,
Wild hideous forms are slowly seen to glide;
She bids them fly to shade earth's brightest blooms,
And spread the blast of Desolation wide.

See! in the darkened air their fiery course!
The sweeping ruin settles o'er the land,
Terror leads on their steps with madd'ning force,
And Death and Vengeance close the ghastly band!

Mark the purple streams that flow!
Mark the deep impassioned woe!
Frantic Fury's dying groan!
Virtue's sigh, and Sorrow's moan!

Wide wide the phantoms swell the loaded air
With shrieks of anguish—madness and despair!
Cease your ruin! specters dire!
Cease your wild terrific sway!
Turn your steps and check your ire,
Yield to peace and mourning day!

~*Superstition, An Ode.*

Then let me stand amidst thy glooms profound
On some wild woody steep, and hear the breeze
That swells in mournful melody around,
And faintly dies upon the distant trees.

What melancholy charm steals o'er the mind!
What hallow'd tears the rising rapture greet!
While many a viewless spirit in the wind
Sighs to the lonely hour in accents sweet!

~ *Night*

William Wordsworth (1770–1850)

Another poet laureate, this one managed to avoid writing official verses proclaiming the virtues of Empire, the weddings of royals, and the ribbon-cutting ceremonies of new railways. Here we sample his contribution to the nineteenth century's idealization of painful discipline.

Stern Daughter of the voice of God!
O Duty! if that name thou love*
Who art a light to guide, a rod
To check the erring, and reprove;
Thou who art victory and law
When empty terrors overawe;
From vain temptations dost set free,
And calm'st the weary strife of frail humanity!

~ *Ode to Duty*

* *shouldn't it be 'lovest' ? Ed.*

Sir Walter Scott (1771–1832)

Scott's day job was to serve as judge and legal administrator. Not content with this sort of paper-shuffling, he composed a wide shelf of very long historical novels, not to mention plays, stories, and poems. All this before the invention of the ball-point pen, still less the word processor, and we can only wonder how much he might have produced if he had had more than a quill pen.

The theme of ghoulish morbidity, pioneered by Ann Radcliffe, is mostly associated with Poe, but Scott could hold his own in the skeleton-clasping field. Following are the final stanzas of a tale of lovers parted by war and facing a grim reunion. Scott may also be the only poet you will find who calls a horse a "barb."

Reluctant on its rusty hinge
  Revolved an iron door,
And by the pale moon's setting beam
  Were seen a church and tower.

With many a shriek and cry, whiz round
  The birds of midnight, scared;
And rustling like autumnal leaves
  Unhallow'd ghosts were heard.

O'er many a tomb and tombstone pale
   He spurr'd the fiery horse,
Till sudden at an open grave
   He checked the wondrous course.

The falling gauntlet quits the rein,
   Down drops the casque of steel,
The cuirass leaves his shrinking side,
   The spur his gory heel.

The eyes desert the naked skull,
   The mould'ring flesh the bone,
Till Helen's lily arms entwine
   A ghastly skeleton.

The furious barb snorts fire and foam,
   And, with a fearful bound,
Dissolves at once in empty air,
   And leaves her on the ground.

Half seen by fits, by fits half heard,
   Pale spectres flit along,
Wheel round the maid in dismal dance
   And howl the funeral song.

~ *William and Helen*

Samuel Taylor Coleridge (1772–1834)

This young man was an idealist in several ways, helping launch the Romantic era in literature and joining with Southey to plan a utopian community in the new world. It was a commune before its time, to be called Pantisocracy (government by all equally). Perhaps the requirement to abandon all personal property (communism, you know) contributed to the collapse of the plan even before the founders had embarked. This defeat did not apparently diminish Coleridge's interest in shipboard life.

> But tell me, tell me! speak again,
> Thy soft response renewing—
> What makes that ship drive on so fast?
> What is the ocean doing?
>
> ~ *Rime of the Ancient Mariner*

Thomas Moore (1779-1852)

This is NOT the Thomas More (1478–1535), the scrupulous churchman who launched the meme that Richard III was a monster. (That More ended his days on the chopping block). This Moore wrote many poems that were later set to music by Berlioz, Ives, Schumann, Britten and others. He lost his faculties at an advanced age and faded gently away.

Oh, breathe not his name! Let it sleep in the shade,
Where cold and unhonored his relics are laid;
Sad, silent and dark be the tears that we shed,
As the night-dew that falls on the grass o'er his head.

...

But the night-dew that falls, though in silence it weeps,
Shall brighten with verdure the grave where he sleeps;
And the tear that we shed, though in secret it rolls,
Shall long keep his memory green in our souls.

~ *Irish Melodies.*

George Gordon, Lord Byron (1786–1824)

Byron single-handedly invented the image of the Romantic poet: handsome, noble, and idealistic enough to join a war of independence, romantically losing his life in the venture. He courted many women and cultivated the impression that he dashed off his verses with carefree spontaneity.

The sun set, and up rose the yellow moon:
   The devil's in the moon for mischief; they
Who call'd her chaste, methinks, began too soon
   Their nomenclature; there is not a day
The longest, not the twenty-first of June,
   Sees half the business in a wicked way
On which three single hours of moonshine smile—
And then she looks so modest all the while.

~ *Don Juan*

O Time! The beautifier of the dead!

~ *Childe Harold's Pilgrimage,* Canto IV

John Keats (1795–1821)

Darn, those Romantic poets died young. We could use so many more sonnets like *On First Looking into Chapman's Homer* and *When I Have Fears That I May Cease to Be.* Having studied medicine and watched his brother die of tuberculosis, he recognized with the first drop of blood that his lung condition would be fatal. Despite the nineteenth century's admiration of languishing heroines, this is not a glamorous way to die. A true romantic, Keats praised nature and yearned for the unattainable past.

> I stood tip-toe upon a little hill,
> The air was cooling and so very still,
> That the sweet buds which with a modest pride
> Pull droopingly, in slanting curve aside,
> That scantly leav'd, and finely tapering stems,
> Had not yet lost those starry diadems
> Caught from the early sobbing of the morn.
>
> ~ *I Stood Tip-Toe Upon a Little Hill*

> Lo! I must tell a tale of chivalry.
>
> ~ *Specimen of an Induction to a Poem*

As if a Naiad, like a meddling elf,
Should darken her pure grot with muddy gloom

~ *On Fame*

… if from shepherd's keep
A lamb stray'd far a-down those inmost glens,
Never again saw he the happy pens
Whither his brethren, bleating with content,
Over the hills at every night-fall went.
…
They stung the feather'd horse: with fierce alarm
He flapped towards the sound.
…
Ask me no more! I may not utter it,
Nor may I be thy love. We might commit
Ourselves at once to vengeance; we might die;
We might embrace and die: voluptuous thought!
Enlarge not to my hunger, or I'm caught
In trammels of perverse deliciousness.
No, no, that shall not be: thee will I bless,
And bid a long adieu.

~ *Endymion*

There came enchantment with the shifting wind,
That did both drown and keep alive my ears.

~ *Hyperion.*

Robert Pollok (1798–1827)

Unknown to our epoch, Pollok was the Milton of his day. His modest opus, *The Course of Time*, illuminated human destiny, consisted (like *Paradise Lost*) of ten very long books, and ran to 25 editions. The last was given to the world 40 years after the author's death. He had managed to compose thousands of lines before his thirtieth birthday, constantly refreshed by a shower of semi-colons. The reader may note in the second selection below a primitive attempt to produce a thesaurus.

Whether in crowds or solitudes, in streets
Or shady groves, dwelt Happiness it seems
In vain to ask; her nature makes it vain,
Tho' poets much, and hermits talked and sung
Of brooks, and crystal founts, and weeping dews
And Myrtle bowers, and solitary vale;
And with the nymph made assignations there;
And wooed her with the love-sick oaten reed;
And sages, too, although less positive,
Advised their sons to court her in the shade.
Delirious babble all!

Will, passion, reason; hopes, fears; joy, distress;
Peace, turbulence; simplicity, deceit;
Good, ill; corruption, immortality;

A temple of the Holy Ghost, and yet
Oft lodging fiends; the dwelling place of all
The heavenly virtues—charity and truth,
Humility, and holiness, and love;
And yet the common haunt of anger, pride
Hatred, revenge, and passions foul with lust;
Allied to heaven, yet parleying oft with hell....
An heir of heaven, and walking thitherward,
Yet casting back a covetous eye on earth;
Emblem of strength, and weakness; loving now,
And now abhorring sin; indulging now,
And now repenting sore; rejoicing now,
With joy unspeakable, and full of glory,
Now weeping bitterly, and clothed in dust.

Good name was dear to all. Without it, none
Could soundly sleep, even on a royal bed,
Or drink with relish from a cup of gold;
...

For honest fame, men laid
Their heads upon the block, and, while the axe
Descended, looked and smiled.

John Greenleaf Whittier (1807–1892)

Dogged devotee of rhythm and rhyme, Whittier dutifully honored the rules of the art. One admires his impassioned campaigning against slavery, but in a poem which is truly worth reading (*The Panorama*), one nevertheless finds this regrettable couplet:

> Give me the heroes who, at tuck of drum,
> Salute thy staff, immortal Quattlebum!

Henry Wadsworth Longfellow (1807–1892)

Descended from some of the earliest English colonists, Longfellow celebrated American history—*The Courtship of Miles Standish, Paul Revere's Ride, The Song of Hiawatha*—poems which are the sources for countless recitations: "Listen, my children, and you shall hear" "Under a spreading chestnut tree" "Speak for yourself, John." Longfellow was the most celebrated poet of his day but is now scorned by critics, to whom I say Faugh! and again, Fie!

The day is cold, and dark, and dreary;
It rains, and the wind is never weary;
The vine still clings to the mouldering wall
And at every gust the dead leaves fall,
  And the day is dark and dreary.

My life is cold, and dark, and dreary;
It rains, and the wind is never weary;
My thoughts still cling to the mouldering Past,
But the hopes of youth fall thick in the blast,
  And the days are dark and dreary.

Be still, sad heart! and cease repining;
Behind the clouds is the sun still shining;
Thy fate is the common fate of all,
Into each life some rain must fall.
  Some days must be dark and dreary.

~ *The Rainy Day*

Edgar Allan Poe (1809–1849)

Poe's own life was worthy of one of his macabre mystery stories. Orphaned by age two, West Point dropout-on-purpose by getting himself court-martialed, marriage that would today be considered indictable (to a cousin aged 13), death from undetermined causes at the age of 40 (all medical records lost), and memory besmirched by his own literary executor. Though he helped invent the detective story, he needed one himself to explain his passing and the callous responses to it. Below, angels and other airy creatures attend a play.

But see, amid the mimic rout
A crawling shape intrude!
A blood-red thing that writhes from out
The scenic solitude!
It writhes! – it writhes! – with mortal pangs
The mimes become its food,
And seraphs sob at vermin fangs
In human gore imbued.

Out—out are the lights—out all!
And, over each quivering form,
The curtain, a funeral pall,
Comes down with the rush of a storm,

While the angels, all pallid and wan,
Uprising, unveiling, affirm
That the play is the tragedy, "Man,"
And its hero the Conqueror Worm.

~ *The Conqueror Worm*

ALFRED LORD TENNYSON (1809–1892)

Like many poets, Tennyson was a parson's son. He showed early promise, and his way with words enriched our language ("Nature, red in tooth and claw" " 'Tis better to have loved and lost than never to have loved at all", "Theirs not to reason why, theirs but to do and die."). After a hiatus caused by intense criticism, he resumed publishing and gained his niche in the hall of fame and the role of Poet Laureate. Tennyson declined to be named a baronet by Disraeli, but was persuaded to become a full baron by Gladstone two decades later. His voice was preserved for us by Thomas Edison on wax cylinders.

In glowing health, with boundless wealth,
  But sickening of a vague disease,
You know so ill to deal with time,
  You needs must play such pranks as these.

~ from *Lady Vere de Vere*

William M. Thackeray (1811–1863)

He should have stuck to novels.

A street there is in Paris famous,
For which no rhyme our language yields,
Rue Neuve des Petits Champs its name is—
The New Street of the Little Fields.

~ *The Ballad of Bouillabaisse*

Robert Browning (1812–1889)

Romantic for his rescue of Elizabeth Barrett from her tyrannical father, and for remaining single the remaining 28 years of his life after she died, Browning ripened into the iconic Victorian poet-sage who inspired poetry societies dedicated to him. However, he was capable of dreadful lapses. *Sordello,* a long and obscure narrative about a 13th-century troubadour, ruined his reputation for years. Tennyson said of it, "There were only two lines in it that I understood, and they were both lies. They were the opening and closing lines: 'Who will may hear Sordello's story told' and 'Who would has heard Sordello's story told.'" Carlyle reported that his wife read it "without being able to make out whether *Sordello* was a man, or a city, or a book." See if you can do better. The first extract below is a single sentence.

> Since, though I might be proud to see the dim
> Abysmal past divide its hateful surge,
> Letting of all men this one man emerge
> Because it pleased me, yet, that moment past,
> I should delight in watching first to last
> His progress as you watch it, not a whit
> More in the secret than yourselves who sit
> Fresh-chapleted to listen.

Confess now, poets know the dragnet's trick,
Catching the dead, if fate denies the quick,
And shaming her; 't is not for fate to choose
Silence or song because she can refuse
Real eyes to glisten more, real hearts to ache
Less oft, real brows turn smoother for our sake:
I have experienced something of her spite;
But there 's a realm wherein she has no right
And I have many lovers. Say; but few
Friends fate accords me? Here they are: now view
The host I muster! Many a lighted face
Foul with no vestige of the grave's disgrace;
What else should tempt them back to taste our air
Except to see how their successors fare?
My audience! and they sit, each ghostly man
Striving to look as living as he can,
Brother by breathing brother; thou art set,
Clear-witted critic, by... but I 'll not fret
A wondrous soul of them, nor move death's spleen
Who loves not to unlock them.

Two Principles that live
Each fitly by its Representative.
"Hill-cat"—who called him so?—the gracefullest
Adventurer, the ambiguous stranger-guest
Of Lombardy (sleek but that ruffling fur,
Those talons to their sheath!) whose velvet purr
Soothes jealous neighbours when a Saxon scout

—Arpo or Yoland, is it?—one without
A country or a name, presumes to couch
Beside their noblest; until men avouch
That, of all Houses in the Trevisan,
Conrad descries no fitter, rear or van,
Than Ecelo!

Browning indulged in other missteps.

Can it be? What, turned melon-seller? Thou?
Clad in such sordid garb, thy seat yon step
Where dogs brush by thee and express contempt?
Methinks, thy head-gear is some scooped-out gourd!

~ *Ferishtah's Fancies*

Let us not explore the lingering question of *how* dogs express contempt, but move along to the rhyme in the following verse.

Meantime, what lights my sunbeam on?
Where settles by degrees the radiant cripple?
Oh, is it surely blown, my martagon?*
New-blown and ruddy as St. Agnes' nipple,
Plump as the flesh-bunch on some Turk bird's poll!

~ *Pippa Passes*

* *martagon = lily*

Walt Whitman (1819–1892)

Whitman was a self-conscious poet, celebrating awareness of his awareness to an extent that the most absorbed of modern psychotherapy patients must admire. He introduced the convention that any sensation or rumination, when put on paper with a ragged right margin, qualifies as poetry. There is such a din of unpoetic language in Whitman's verse—adhesiveness, efflux, scrofula—that it is hard to believe that he was once admired by Emerson. Yet the true lover of bad verse must be grateful, for Whitman has left us reams of pleasure.

I celebrate myself, and sing myself;
And what I assume you shall assume,
For every atom belonging to me as good belongs to you
...

The sharp-hoof'd moose of the north,
  the cat on the house-sill,
The chickadee, the prairie-dog,
The litter of the grunting sow as they tug at her teats,
The brood of the turkey-hen and she with her
  half-spread wings,
I see in them and myself the same old law.

~ *Song of Myself*

Down, down, proud gorge!—though choking thee,
Thy bearded throat and high-borne forehead to the
gutter;
Crouch low thy neck to eleemosynary* gifts.

~ *To the Pending Year*

* *eleemosynary = pertaining to charity. What is this word doing here? – Ed.*

O how shall I warble myself for the dead one there
I have loved?
And how shall I deck my song for the large sweet soul
that has gone?
And what shall my perfume be for the grave of him
I love?

~ *When Lilacs Last in the Dooryard Bloom'd*

Here is the efflux of the soul.

~ *Song of the Open Road*

Matthew Arnold (1822–1888)

School administrators rarely make history, but Arnold, son of a Rugby headmaster, was a school inspector for 35 years. This career seems not to have crushed his creativity; perhaps his friendship with Wordsworth helped keep his muse alive. Luckily, he moved past his early assemblage (*Empedocles on Etna)* and, despite becoming a professor, rose to the heights of *Dover Beach*. And yet there's this:

Go, for they call you, shepherd, from the hill;
  Go, shepherd, and untie the wattled cotes!*
    No longer leave thy wistful flock unfed,
  Nor let the bawling fellows wrack their throats
    Nor the cropped herbage shoot another head.

~ *The Scholar-Gypsy*

* *cote = pen for animals*

Anonymous

Supposedly dictated by Poe's ghost to this unknown mediumistic scribe, this poem echoes *The Raven* and, though purportedly from a woman, seems to be a cry from Poe himself from the great Beyond, since he himself had died delirious in mysterious circumstances in Baltimore. Five additional stanzas bring this transmission to a poignant close.

Woman weak and woman mortal, through the
  spirit's open portal,
I would read the Punic record of mine earthly being
  o'er—
I would feel that fire returning which within my soul
  was burning
When my star was quenched in darkness,
  set to rise on earth no more,
When I sank beneath Life's burdens in the streets
  of Baltimore.

Ah. those memories sore and saddening! Ah, that
  night of anguish maddening!
When my lone heart suffered shipwreck on a
  demon-haunted shore—

When the fiends grew wild with laughter,
  and the silence following after
Was more awful and appalling than the
  cannon's deadly roar—
Than the tramp of mighty armies
  thro' the streets of Baltimore.

~ *Streets of Baltimore,* circa 1859.

Horatio Alger (1832–1899)

A hundred Alger novels tell variations on the theme of "poor boy makes good"—always with the help of a kind older man. Alger's first big hit, *Ragged Dick: or, Street Life in New York with the Boot Blacks,* rejoices in the good fortune of a shoe-shine boy rewarded for his honesty and good deeds, especially for rescuing a drowning child. By this time, Alger had been publishing poems for nearly twenty years, a form he returned to in his life's work of praising virtue. In the poem extracted here, a heroic helmsman steers a burning ship to shore.

"John Maynard!" with an anxious voice
   The captain cries once more,
"Stand by the wheel five minutes yet,
   And we shall reach the shore."
Through flame and smoke that dauntless heart
   Responded firmly still,
Unawed, though face to face with death,
   "With God's good help I will."

The flames approach with giant strides,
   They search his hand and brow;
One arm, disabled, seeks his side,
   Ah! he is conquered now.

But no, his teeth are firmly set,
  He crushes down his pain;
His knee upon the stanchion pressed,
  He guides the ship again.

One moment yet! one moment yet!
  Brave heart, thy task is o'er;
The pebbles grate beneath the keel
  The steamer touches shore.
Three hundred grateful voices rise
  In praise to God that he
Hath saved them from the fearful fire,
  And from the engulfing sea.

But where is he, that helmsman bold?
  The captain saw him reel;
His nerveless hands released their task;
  He sank beside the wheel.
The wave received his lifeless corse,
  Blackened with smoke and fire.
God rest him! Never hero had
  A nobler funeral pyre!

~ *John Maynard: A Ballad of Lake Erie*

James Whitcomb Riley (1849–1916)

Balladeer of the bucolic life, hymnodist of humble homes, Riley was sporadically educated, and it shows. He achieved fame late in life (his portrait was painted by Sargent) and was mourned by the nation, including Woodrow Wilson.

Pap's got his patent right, and rich as all creation;
  But where's the peace and comfort that we all had had before?
Let's go a-visitin' back to Griggsby's Station—
  Back where we ust to be so happy and so pore!

The likes of us a-living' here! It's just a mortal pity
  To see us in this great big house with carpets on the stairs
And the pump right in the kitchen! And the city, city, city!
  And nothin' but the city around us everywhere.

Climb clean above the roof and look out from the steeple,
  And never see a robin, nor a beech nor elm tree!
Right there in earshot of at least a thousand people,
  And none that neighbors with us, or we want to go and see.

Let's go a-visitin' back go Griggsby's Station—
  Back where the latch-string's a-hanging' from the door,
And every neighbor around the place as dear as a relation—
  Back where we ust to be so happy and so pore!

~ *Back to Griggsby's Station*

Thomas Stearns Eliot (1888–1965)

Seldom has a banker made such good use of his weekends. Eliot was apparently good at his day job. A highly placed official at his branch told critic I.A. Richards that he approved of the young man's poetry "hobby" because "I think it helps him with his work. If you see our young friend, you might tell him that we think he's doing quite well at the Bank. In fact, if he goes on as he has been doing, I don't see why – in time, of course, in time — he mightn't even become a Branch Manager."

They are rattling breakfast plates in basement kitchens,
And along the trampled edges of the street
I am aware of the damp souls of housemaids
Sprouting despondently at area gates.

~ *Morning at the Window*

As she laughed I was aware of becoming involved
in her laughter and being part of it,
    until her teeth were only
accidental stars with a talent for squad-drill.

~ *Hysteria*

The readers of the *Boston Evening Transcript*
Sway in the wind like a field of ripe corn.
When evening quickens faintly in the street,
Wakening the appetites of life in some
And to others bringing the *Boston Evening Transcript*,
I mount the steps and ring the bell, turning
Wearily, as one would turn to nod good-bye to
    Rochefoucauld,
If the street were time and he at the end of the street,
And I say, "Cousin Harriet, here is the *Boston Evening*
    Transcript."

~ *The Boston Evening Transcript*

John Crowe Ransom (1888–1974)

One of those polymath poets who moonlight as critics, scholars, professors, and editors, Ransom practiced rhyme and rhythm, as we see in the selections below.

Beautifully Janet slept
Till it was deeply morning. She woke then
And thought about her dainty-feathered hen,
To see how it had kept.

One kiss she gave her mother,
Only a small one gave she to her daddy
Who would have kissed each curl of his shining baby;
No kiss at all for her brother.

"Old Chucky, Old Chucky!" she cried,
Running across the world upon the grass
To Chucky's house, and listening. But alas,
Her Chucky had died.

It was a transmogrifying bee
Came droning down on Chucky's old bald head
And sat and put the poison. It scarcely bled,

But how exceedingly
And purply* did the knot
Swell with the venom and communicate
Its rigour! Now the poor comb stood up straight
But Chucky did not.

~ *Janet Waking*

* *"purply"? – Ed.*

The little cousin is dead, by foul subtraction,
A green bough for Virginia's aged tree,
And none of the country kin like the transaction,
Nor some of the world of outer dark, like me.

~ *Dead Boy*

And now, the twentieth century, in brief

(Biographical notes are not given for those born after 1900.)

Randall Jarrell (1914–1965)

In a fashionable suburb of Santa Barbara,
Montecito, there visited me one night at midnight
a scream with breasts.
...
Her seat at the cricket matches
is warmed by buttocks less delectable than hers.
Greenie's girdle is empty.

~ *In Montecito*

Robert Layzor (unknown)

But the girls come and sprinkle
The lavender of their hearts
On the gasping red piazza
Where the young men play darts.

~ *Saint's Parade*

Richard Hugo (1923–1982)

Green tons hold you down, and ten bass curve
teasing in your hair. Summer slime
will pile deep on your breast
...
I hope each spring
to find you tangled in those pads ...
star in dead reflection off your teeth ...
already faded, lover, where you bloat.

~ *The Lady in Kicking Horse Reservoir*

John Ashbery (1927–2017)

I learned that you called for me. I came to where
you were living, up a stair. There was no one there.
No one to appreciate me. The legality of it upset a chair.

~ *The New Higher*

John Hollander (1929–2013)

Too soon, too soon, he plunges
His hand under the mound
Of taffeta around her!

~ *Paysage Moralisé*

Donald Finkel (1929–2008)

The poem makes truth a little more disturbing,
like a good bra, lifts it and holds it out in both hands.

~ *Hands*

Intermission

Poets are not the only ones who make aesthetic missteps. Playwrights have dutifully contributed their share to literary hilarity. Shakespeare hinted that composing bad poetry might even be hazardous. His play *Julius Caesar* depicts the aftermath of the assassination of the title character (who bites the dust in Act III). A poet named Cinna is mistaken by the enraged and violent mob for Cinna the conspirator.

First citizen: Tear him to pieces. He's a conspirator.

Cinna the poet: I am Cinna the *poet,* I am Cinna the *poet.*

Fourth citizen: Tear him for his bad verses! Tear him for his bad verses!

Some authors better known as poets attempted the dramatic form, as seen below. Before enjoying some dreadful dialogue, let us give playwrights credit for giving their characters sprightly names. Jacobean playwrights contrived such elegances as Brainworm,[1] Sir Giles Overreach,[2] and Supervacuo.[3] Later in that century, Restoration comedy gave us Sir Fopling Flutter,[4] Sir Jasper Fidget, and Mrs. Squeamish.[5] The 18th century is renowned for Sir Benjamin Backbite and Lady Sneerwell.[6] As late as the mid-19th century, we acquired Lady Gay Spanker.[7]

This droll tradition must be revived. Having completed her labors over the present contribution to Western civilization, the editor might indulge in a drama with the characters Sir Standwell Back (pompous but cowardly nobleman), Marginalia (a sweet, slightly irrelevant ingenue), Grendelette (a reformed governess), and the Teutonic braggart soldiers Pickelhaube and Dudelsack.[8]

---

1. Jonson, *Every Man in his Humor*
2. Massinger, *A New Way to Pay Old Debts*
3. Middleton, *The Revenger's Tragedy*
4. George Etherege, *The Man of Mode*
5. Wycherly, *The Country Wife*
6. Sheridan, *The School for Scandal*
7. Dion Boucicault, *London Assurance*
8. German for "pointed helmet" and "bagpipes," respectively.

CYRIL TOURNEUR (1575–1626)
The Atheist's Tragedy

Tourneur was one of the playwrights who made the epithet "Jacobean" a byword for bloody finales, with the stage littered with more bodies than in *Hamlet.* These two lovers, however, survive.

Castabella. O the sad trouble of my fearful soul!
My faithful servant, did you never hear
That when a certain great man went to the war,
The lovely face of Heaven was masqued with sorrow,
The sighing winds did move the breast of earth,
The heavy clouds hung down their mourning heads,
And wept sad showers the day that he went hence
As if that day presaged some ill success
That fatally should kill his happiness.
And so it came to pass. Methinks my eyes
(Sweet Heaven forbid!) are like those weeping clouds,
And as their showers presaged, so do my tears.
Some sad event will follow my sad fears.

Charlemont. Fie, superstitions! Is it bad to kiss?

Castabella. May all my fears hurt me no more than this!

Thomas Heywood (1572?–1641)
A Woman Killed with Kindness

Shakespeare's younger contemporary was likewise a prolific playwright, actor, and part owner of his theatre company. He seemed preoccupied with domestic affairs, judging by his plays *How a Man May Choose a Good Wife from a Bad, A Maidenhead Well Lost,* and *Swetnam the Woman-Hater.* In this domestic tragedy, considered Heywood's masterpiece, adultery leads to the womanly virtue of self-starvation.

Wendoll. The path of pleasure and the gate to bliss,
Which on your lips I knock at with a kiss!
...Your husband's from home, your bed's no blab.
Nay, look not down and blush!

After overcoming her blushes and cavorting with Wendoll, Anne is caught in the act and banished by her husband. She takes remorse to extremes.

Mrs. Frankford. Oh me, base strumpet,
That, having such a husband, such sweet children,
Must enjoy neither! Oh, to redeem mine honour,
I'd have this hand cut off, these my breasts sear'd;
Be rack'd, strappado'd, put to any torment:
Nay, to whip but this scandal out, I'd hazard
The rich and dear redemption of my soul!
He cannot be so base as to forgive me,

Nor I so shameless to accept his pardon.
Oh, women, women, you that yet have kept
Your holy matrimonial vow unstain'd,
Make me your instance; when you tread awry,
Your sins, like mine, will on your conscience lie.

Later:
Mrs. Frankford. [to servant]
If you return unto my master, say
(Though not from me, for I am all unworthy
To blast his name so with a strumpet's tongue)
That you have seen me weep, wish myself dead!
Nay, you may say, too (for my vow is past),
Last night you saw me eat and drink my last.
This to your master you may say and swear;
For it is writ in heaven, and decreed here.

JOHN DRYDEN (1631–1700)
All for Love; or, The World Well Lost

Dryden distinguished himself in formal verse and in drama for the stage. Thwarted lovers, mistaken identities, and other worn plot devices mark his comic success, *Marriage à la Mode*. In a more serious vein, he dared to tell the story of Antony and Cleopatra (*All for Love*), and remarkably, his version was preferred to Shakespeare's for much of the eighteenth century. Its success was probably not due to his antagonistic prologue, which begins:

What flocks of critics hover here to-day,
As vultures wait on armies for their prey,
All gaping for the carcass of a play!
With croaking notes they bode some dire event,
And follow dying poets by the scent.

Dryden's play begins with portents and prodigies, which are familiar from Shakespeare's Roman plays. An observant citizen has noticed them.

Forsaken dolphins there with their broad tails,
Lay lashing the departing waves: hard by them,
Sea horses floundering in the slimy mud,
Tossed up their heads, and dashed the ooze
  about them.

A political marriage (Antony to Caesar's sister Octavia) becomes love on her part, and she begs him to leave Cleopatra. He resists her pleas until this touching scene, complete with winsome children:

Octavia. Come, come, my lord, if I can pardon you,
Methinks you should accept it. Look on these;
Are they not yours? or stand they thus neglected,
As they are mine? Go to him, children, go;
Kneel to him, take him by the hand, speak to him;
For you may speak, and he may own you too,
Without a blush; and so he cannot all
His children: go, I say, and pull him to me,
And pull him to yourselves, from that bad woman.
You, Agrippina, hang upon his arms;
And you, Antonia, clasp about his waist:
If he will shake you off, if he will dash you
Against the pavement, you must bear it, children;
For you are mine, and I was born to suffer.
[*The children go to him*]

Octavia. Husband!

Children. Father!*

Antony. I am vanquished: take me,
Octavia; take me, children; share me all.

* *Tears on all sides. – Ed.*

Dryden was unable to resist the lure of inventing a scene in which Cleopatra meets her rival. Mutual derision ensues, too elevated in tone to be considered a jealous slanging match.

Octavia. Shame of our sex,
Dost thou not blush to own those black endearments,
That make sin pleasing?

Cleopatra. You may blush, who lack them.
If bounteous nature, if indulgent Heaven
Have given me charms to please the bravest man,
Should I not thank them? Should I be ashamed,
And not be proud? I am, that he has loved me;
And, when I love not him, Heaven change this face
For one like yours.

George Gordon, Lord Byron (1788–1824)

Manfred: A Dramatic Poem

A despairing scholar, not unlike Marlowe's Faustus, denounces his studies as worthless and calls up spirits from the deep. His entreaty summons not one but seven treacherous spirits.

The star which rules thy destiny
Was ruled, ere earth began, by me:
It was a world as fresh and fair
As e'er revolved round un in air;
Its course was free and regular,
Space bosom'd* not a lovelier star.
The hour arrived—and it became
A wandering mass of shapeless flame,
A pathless comet, and a curse,
The menace of the universe;
Still rolling on with innate force,
Without a sphere, without a course,
A bright deformity on high,
The monster of the upper sky!

* *"bosom'd" ? – Ed.*

Quoted in Isaac D'Israeli's *Curiosities of Literature*

The elder D'Israeli was a scholar whose most popular work, *Curiosities of Literature,* reached eleven editions in his lifetime. His son, Prime Minister Benjamin Disraeli, removed the apostrophe and found time apart from his political obligations to carry on the family literary bent in novels, poems, and a play. Neither father nor son perpetrated the following. It definitely qualifies as a "curiosity."

Friend. Most learned cook, who can observe these canons?

Master Cook. And therefore phlegm and colic make a man
A most indecent guest. The aliment
Dress'd in my kitchen is true aliment;
Light of digestion easily it passes;
The chyle soft-blending from the juicy food
Repairs the solids.

Friend. Ah! The Chyle! the solids!
Thou new Democritus! thou sage of medicine!

Christopher Fry (1907–2005)

A Phoenix Too Frequent

Long-lived Fry wrote one of the finest plays of the 20th century, *The Lady's Not for Burning,* and I'm not the only one who thinks so. It was performed at the National Theatre in 2001 as one of the century's 100 best. His plays were performed by the cream of English actors and directors and he also wrote for movies, including *Ben-Hur* (uncredited) and other toga epics.

Tegeus. Here in a grave, separate from any life,
I and the only one of beauty, the only
Persuasive key to all my senses,
In spite of having lain day after day
And pored upon the sepals, corolla, stamen and bracts
Of the yellow bog-iris—

Dynamene. I have never
Been greatly moved by the yellow bog-iris.

Edgar Allan Poe

Politian

We must imagine that our hero, named Politian, is the Earl of Leicester (!), visiting childhood friend Baldazzar in Rome. Upstairs, fair maid Lalage sings a lament.

Politian. What voice was that?

Baldazzar. I heard it not.
I heard not any voice except thine own,
And the echo of thine own.

Politian. Then I but dreamed.

Baldazzar. Give not thy soul to dreams:
the camp, the court
Befit thee—Fame awaits thee—Glory calls—
And her the trumpet-tongued thou wilt not hear
In hearkening to imaginary sounds
And phantom voices.

Politian. It is a phantom voice!
Didst not thou not hear it then?

Baldazzar. I heard it not.

Politian. Thou heardst it not!—Baldazzar, speak no more
To me, Politian, of thy camps and courts.
Oh! I am sick, sick, sick, even unto death,

Of the hollow and high-sounding vanities
Of the populous Earth! Bear with me yet a while!
We have been boys together—school-fellows—
And now are friends—yet shall not be so long—
For in the eternal city thou shalt do me
A kind and gentle office, and a Power—
A Power august, benignant, and supreme—
Shall then absolve thee of all farther duties
Unto thy friend.

Baldazzar. Thou speakest a fearful riddle
I will not understand.*

Politian. Yet now as Fate
Approaches, and the Hours are breathing low,
The sands of Time are changed to golden grains
And dazzle me, Baldazzar. Alas! alas!
I cannot die, having within my heart
So keen a relish for the beautiful
As has been kindled within it. Methinks the air
Is balmier now than it was wont to be—
Rich melodies are floating in the winds—
A rarer loveliness bedecks the earth
And with a holier lustre the quiet moon
Sitteth in heaven. Hist! hist! thou canst not say
Thou hearest not now, Baldazzar?

Baldazzar. Indeed I hear not.

* *We won't either. – Ed.*

Politian. Not hear it!—listen now—listen!
—the faintest sound
and yet the sweetest ever heard!
A lady's voice!—and sorrow in the tone!
Baldazzar, it oppresses me like a spell!
Again!—again!—how solemnly it falls
Into my heart of hearts! That eloquent voice
Surely I never heard—yet it were well
Had I but heard it with its thrilling tones
In earlier days!

Baldazzar. I myself hear it now.
Be still!—the voice, if I mistake not greatly
Proceeds from yonder lattice—which you may see
Very plainly through the window—it belongs
Does it not? unto this palace of the Duke.

Poe's regrettable addiction to dashes and exclamation marks blights what is otherwise a plaintive and touching drama, taking place in a chamber through whose window yonder lattice may plainly be spied.

Edmond Rostand

Cyrano de Bergerac

The verse drama *Cyrano de Bergerac* is his monument, an immediate success onstage and revived in many forms, but Rostand also wrote a play (*Les Romanesques*) that was part of the source material for Harvey Schmidt and Tom Jones's marvelous 1960 musical, *The Fantasticks.* I know not whether *Cyrano* sounds as ridiculous in the original French, but we can enjoy the following four passages in translation.

Cyrano: Fat man, take warning! If you go on, I
Shall feel myself constrained to cuff your face!

The marquis: Have done!

Cyrano: And if these lords hold not their tongue
Shall feel constrained to make them taste my cane!

...

The Viscount (choking with rage): Hear his arrogance!
A country lout who ... who ... has got no gloves!
Who goes out without sleeve-knots, ribbons, lace!

Cyrano: True; all my elegances are within.
I do not prank myself out, puppy-like;
My toilet is more thorough, if less gay;

I would not sally forth—a half-washed-out
Affront upon my cheek—a conscience
Yellow-eyed, bilious, from its sodden sleep,
A ruffled honor,. . .scruples grimed and dull!
I show no bravery of shining gems.
Truth, Independence, are my fluttering plumes.
'Tis not my form I lace to make me slim,
But brace my soul with efforts as with stays,
Covered with exploits, not with ribbon-knots,
My spirit bristling high like your mustaches,
I, traversing the crowds and chattering groups
Make Truth ring bravely out like clash of spurs!

...

Cyrano: Look well at me—then tell me, with what hope
This vile protuberance can inspire my heart!
I do not lull me with illusions—yet
At times I'm weak: in evening hours dim
I enter some fair pleasance, perfumed sweet;
With my poor ugly devil of a nose
I scent spring's essence—in the silver rays
I see some knight—a lady on his arm,
And think 'To saunter thus 'neath the moonshine,
I were fain to have my lady, too, beside!'
Thought soars to ecstasy. . .O sudden fall!
—The shadow of my profile on the wall!

...

Cyrano: A kiss, when all is said,—what is it?
An oath that's ratified,—a sealed promise,
A heart's avowal claiming confirmation,—
A rose-dot on the 'i' of 'adoration,'—
A secret that to mouth, not ear, is whispered,—
Brush of a bee's wing, that makes time eternal,—
Communion perfumed like the spring's wild flowers,—
The heart's relieving in the heart's outbreathing,
When to the lips the soul's flood rises, brimming!

T.S. Eliot, *Murder in the Cathedral*

Even a Nobel prize winner can falter. An odd but strangely effective rendering of ominous atmosphere, this play is an intellectual debate about Thomas à Becket in his struggle against King Henry II: Is he a goodie or a baddie? A chorus of Canterbury locals is mystified and not afraid to say so.

Chorus: What is the sickly smell, the vapour?
The dark green light from a cloud on a withered tree?
The earth is heaving to parturition of issue of hell.
What is the sticky dew that forms on the back of
    my hands?
...

I have smelt them, the death-bringers, senses are
    quickened
By subtle forebodings; I have heard
Fluting in the night-time, fluting and owls, have seen
    at noon
Scaly wings slanting over, huge and ridiculous. I have
    tasted
The savour of putrid flesh in the spoon ... I have tasted
The living lobster, the crab, the oyster, the whelk
    and the prawn;
And they live and spawn in my bowels,
And my bowels dissolve in the light of dawn.

The Compleat Mischief

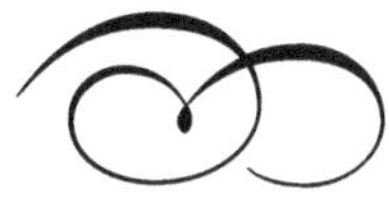

We can best enjoy poetical misdemeanors in their full settings, so below the editor has placed complete poems.

Mary Sidney, Countess of Pembroke

The selection below seems a rather tactless praise of a Greek goddess who was known, like the Queen, for her virginity.

A Dialogue between two shepherds, *Thenot* and *Piers, in praise of* Astrea, *made by the excellent Lady, the Lady* Mary, *Countess of Pembroke, at the Queen's Majesty's being at her house at* ———, *Anno 15* ———.

Thenot. I sing divine *Astrea*'s praise,
O Muses! help my wits to raise,
And heave my Verses higher.

Piers. Thou need'st the truth but plainly tell,
Which much I doubt thou canst not well,
Thou art so oft a lier.

Thenot. If in my Song no more I show,
Than Heav'n, and Earth, and Sea do know,
Then truly I have spoken.

Piers. Sufficeth not no more to name,
But being no less, the like, the same,
Else laws of truth be broken.

Thenot. Then say, she is so good, so fair,
With all the earth she may compare,
Not Momus self denying.

Piers. Compare may think where likeness holds,
Nought like to her the earth enfolds,
I lookt to find you lying.

Thenot. Astrea sees with Wisdom's sight,
Astrea works by Virtue's might,
And jointly both do stay in her.

Piers. Nay take from them, her hand, her mind,
The one is lame, the other blind
Shall still you lying stain her?

Thenot. Soon as *Astrea* shows her face,
Straight every ill avoids the place,
And every good aboundeth.

Piers. Nay long before her face doth show,
The last doth come, the first doth go,
How loud this lie resoundeth!

Thenot. Astrea is our chiefest joy,
Our chiefest guard against annoy,
Our chiefest wealth, our treasure,

Piers. Where chiefest are, there others be,
To us none else, but only she;
When wilt thou speak in measure?

Thenot. Astrea may be justly said,
A field in flow'ry robe arrayed,
In season freshly springing.

Piers. That Spring endures but shortest time,
This never leaves *Astrea's* clime,
Thou liest, instead of singing.

Thenot. As heavenly light that guides the day,
Right so doth thine each lovely ray,
That from *Astrea* flyeth.

Piers. Nay, darkness oft that light enclouds,
Astrea's beam no darkness shrowds;
How loudly *Thenot* lieth!

Thenot. *Astrea* rightly term I may,
A manly Palm, a maiden Bay,
Her verdure never dying.

Piers. Palm oft is crooked, Bay is low,
She still upright, still high doth grow,
Good *Thenot* leave thy lying.

Thenot. Then *Piers*, of friendship tell me why,
My meaning true, my words should lye,
And strive in vain to raise her?

Piers. Words from conceit do only rise,
Above conceit her honor flies,
But silence, nought can praise her.

Ann Radcliffe

When first the vernal morn of life,
  Beam'd on my infant eye,
Fond I survey'd the smiling scene,
  Nor saw the tempest nigh,

Hope's bright illusions touch'd my soul,
  My young ideas led;
And Fancy's vivid tints combined,
  And fairy prospects spread.

My guileless heart expanded wide,
  With filial fondness fraught;
Paternal love that heart supplied
  With all its fondness sought.

But O! the cruel, quick reverse!
  Fate all I lov'd involv'd;
Pale Grief Hope's trembling rays dispers'd,
  And Fancy's dreams dissolv'd.

~ from the novel
Castles of Athlin and Dunbaye

Slow o'er the Apennine, with bleeding feet,
A patient Pilgrim wound his lonely way,
To deck the Lady of Loretto's seat
With all the little wealth his zeal could pay.
From mountain-tops cold died the ev'ning ray,
And, stretch'd in twilight, slept the vale below;
And now the last, last purple streaks of day
Along the melancholy West fade slow.
High o'er his head, the restless pines complain,
As on their summit rolls the breeze of night;
Beneath, the hoarse stream chides the rocks in vain:
The Pilgrim pauses on the dizzy height.
Then to the vale his cautious step he prest,
For there a hermit's cross was dimly seen,
Cresting the rock, and there his limbs might rest,
Cheer'd in the good man's cave, by faggot's sheen,
On leafy beds, nor guile his sleep molest.
Unhappy Luke! he trusts a treacherous clue!
Behind the cliff the lurking robber stood;
No friendly moon his giant shadow threw
Athwart the road, to save the Pilgrim's blood;
On as he went a vesper-hymn he sang,
The hymn, that nightly sooth'd him to repose.
Fierce on his harmless prey the ruffian sprang!
The Pilgrim bleeds to death, his eye-lids close,
Yet his meek spirit knew no vengeful care,
But, dying, for his murd'rer breath'd—a sainted pray'r!"

~ *The Pilgrim,* from *The Mysteries of Udolpho*

Thackeray
Little Billee

There were three sailors of Bristol city
Who took a boat and went to sea;
But first with beef and captain's biscuits
And pickled pork they loaded she.

There was gorging Jack and guzzling Jimmy,
And the youngest he was little Billee.
Now when they got as far as the Equator
They'd nothing left but one split pea.

Says gorging Jack to guzzling Jimmy,
"I am extremely hungaree."
To gorging Jack says guzzling Jimmy,
"We've nothing left, us must eat we."

Says gorging Jack to guzzling Jimmy,
"With one another we shouldn't agree!
There's little Bill, he's young and tender;
We're old and tough, so let's eat he.

"Oh Billy, we're going to kill and eat you,
So undo the button of your chemie."
When Bill received this information
He used his pocket handkerchie.

"First let me say my catechism,
Which my poor mammy taught to me."
"Make haste, make haste," says guzzling Jimmy,
While Jack pulled out his snickersnee.

So Billy went up to the main-top-gallant-mast,
And down he fell on his bended knee.
He scarce had come to the twelfth commandment
When up he jumps. "There's land I see—

"Jerusalem and Madagascar
And North and South Amerikee;
There's the British flag a-riding at anchor,
With Admiral Napier, K.C.B."

So when they got aboard of the Admiral's,
He hanged fat Jack and flogged Jimmee;
But as for little Bill he made him
The Captain of a Seventy-three."

Browning

Soliloquy of the Spanish Cloister

My Last Duchess showed that Browning could deliver a masterful soliloquy. Perhaps this was a trial run at that genre.

Gr-r-r—there go, my heart's abhorrence!
   Water your damned flower-pots, do!
If hate killed men, Brother Lawrence,
   God's blood, would not mine kill you!
What? your myrtle bush wants trimming?
   Oh, that rose has prior claims—
Needs its leaden vase filled brimming?
   Hell dry you up with its flames!

At the meal we sit together:
   Salve tibi! I must hear
Wise talk of the kind of weather,
   Sort of season, time of year:
Not a plenteous cork-crop: scarcely
   Dare we hope oak-galls, I doubt?
What's the Latin name for 'parsley'?
   What's the Greek name for Swine's Snout?

Whew! We'll have our platter burnished,
   Laid with care on our own shelf!
With a fire-new spoon we're furnished,
   And a goblet for ourself,

Raised like something sacrificial
   Ere 'tis fit to touch our chaps—
Marked with L, for our initial!
   (hee, hee! There his lily snaps!)

Saint, forsooth! While brown Dolores
   Squats outside the Convent bank,
With Sanchicha, telling stories
   Steeping tresses in the tank,
Blue-black, lustrous, thick like horsehairs,
   Can't I see his dead eye glow
Bright, as 'twere a Barbary corsair'd?
   (That is, if he'd let it show!)

When he finishes refection,
   Knife and fork he never lays
Cross-wise, to my recollection
   As do I, in Jesu's praise.
I the Trinity illustrate
   Drinking watered orange-pulp—
In three sips the Arian frustrate;
   While he drains his at one gulp!

Oh, those melons! If he's able
   We're to have a feast; so nice!
One goes to the Abbot's table,
All of us to get each a slice.
How go on your flowers? None double?
   Not one fruit-sort can you spy?

Strange! And I, too, at such trouble
Keep ‘em close-nipped on the sly!

There’s a great text in Galatians,
Once you trip on it, entails
Twenty-nine distinct damnations,
One sure, if another fails.
If I trip him just a-dying,
Sure of Heaven as sure can be,
Spin him round and send him flying
Off to Hell, a Manichee?

Or, my scrofulous French novel,
On grey paper with blunt type!
Simply glance at it, you grovel
Hand and foot in Belial’s gripe:
If I double down its pages
At the woeful sixteenth print
When he gathers his greengages
Ope a sieve and slip it in’t?

Or there’s Satan! –-one might venture
Pledge one’s soul to him, yet leave
Such a flaw in the indenture
As he’d miss till, past retrieve,
Blasted lay that rose-acacia
We’re so proud of! *Hy, Zy, Hine,*
Ssst, there’s Vespers! *Plena gratia,*
Ave Virgo, Gr-r-r—you swine!

H. C. Bunner

Behold the Deeds!

In his day, Bunner was known for his short stories and sketches, though he also committed a play entitled *Tower of Babel* and poems like the one below.

I would that all men my hard case might know;
  How grievously I suffer for no sin:
I, Adolphe Culpepper Ferguson, for lo!
  I of my landlady am locked in.
For being short on this sad Saturday,
Nor having shekels of silver wherewith to pay,
She has turned and is departed with my key;
Wherefore, not even as other boarders free,
I sing (as prisoners to their dungeon stones
When for ten days they expiate a spree):
  Behold the deeds that are done of Mrs. Jones!

One night and one day have I wept my woe;
  Nor wot I when the morrow doth begin,
If I shall have to write to Briggs & Co.,
  To pray them to advance the requisite tin
For ransom of their salesman, that he may
Go forth as other boarders go always—
As these I hear now flocking from their tea,
Led by the daughter of my landlady

Pianoward. This day for all my moans,
Dry bread and water have been served me,
Behold the deeds that are done of Mrs. Jones!

Miss Annabel Jones is musical, and so
The heart of the young he-boarder doth win,
Playing "The Maiden's Prayer," adagio—
That fetcheth him, as fetcheth the banco skin
The innocent rustic. For my part, I pray,
That Badarjewska maid may wait for aye
Ere sits she with a lover, as did we
Once sit together, Annabel! Can it be
That all of that arduous wooing not atones
For Saturday shortness of trad dollars three?
Behold the deeds that are done of Mrs. Jones!

Yea! she forgets the arm was wont to go
Around her waist. She wears a buckle whose pin
Galleth the crook of the young man's elbow;
I forget not, for I that youth have been.
Smith was aforetime the Lotharios gay.
Yet once, I mind me, Smith was forced to stay
Close in his room. Not calm, as I, was he;
But his noise brought no pleasaunce, verily.
Small ease he gat of playing on the bones,
Or hammering on his stove-pipe, that I see.
Behold the deeds that are done of Mrs. Jones!

Thou, for whose fear the figurative crow
  I eat, accursed be thou and all thy kin!
Thee will I show up—yea, up will I show
  Thy too thick buckwheats, and thy tea too thin.
Ay! Here I dare thee, ready for the fray!
Thou dost not keep a first-class house, I say!
It does not with the advertisements agree.
Thou lodgest a Briton with a puggaree,*
  And thou hast harbored Jacobses and Cohns,
Also a Mulligan. Thus denounce I thee!
  Behold the deeds that are done of Mrs. Jones!

Envoy**

Boarders! the worst I have not told to ye:
She hath stole my trousers, that I may not flee
  Privily by the window. Hence these groans,
There is no fleeing in a *robe de nuit.*
  Behold the deeds that are done of Mrs. Jones!

* *puggaree = turban*

** *He means envoi. – Ed.*

William Cowper

The Diverting History of John Gilpin

Cowper wrote hymns as well as secular verse. His poem *Light Shining out of Darkness* gave English the phrase, "God moves in a mysterious way His wonders to perform." It is conjectured that the following poem was intended to be comical.

John Gilpin was a citizen
  Of credit and renown,
A train-band captain eke was he
  Of famous London town.

John Gilpin's spouse said to her dear,
  "Though wedded we have been
These twice ten tedious years, yet we
  No holiday have seen.

"Tomorrow is our wedding-day,
  And we shall then repair
Unto the Bell at Edmonton,
  All in a chaise and pair.

"My sister, and my sister's child,
Myself and children three,
Will fill the chaise; so you must ride
  On horseback after we."

He soon replied, "I do admire
  Of womankind but one
And you are she, my dearest dear,
  Therefore it shall be done.

"I am a linen-draper bold,
  As all the world doth know,
And my good friend the calender
  Will lend his horse to go."

Quoth Mrs. Gilpin, "That's well said;
  And for that wine is dear,
We will be furnished with our own
Which is both bright and clear."

John Gilpin kissed his loving wife;
  O'erjoyed was he to find,
That though on pleasure she was bent
  She had a frugal mind.

This captivating history continues at great length. We leave our hero clinging to a runaway horse, hat and wig blown off and left far behind.

Wordsworth

Reverie of Poor Susan

Wordsworth is perhaps the best incarnation of the "keep writing and the idea will come" school of poetry.

At the corner of Wood Street, when daylight appears,
Hangs a Thrush that sings loud, it has sung
 for three years:
Poor Susan has pass'd by the spot, and has heard
In the silence of morning the song of the bird.

'Tis a note of enchantment; what ails her? She sees
A mountain ascending, a vision of trees;
Bright volumes of vapour through Lothbury glide,
And a river flows on through the vale of Cheapside.

Green pastures she views in the midst of the dale
Down which she so often has tripp'd with her pail;
And a single small cottage, a nest like a dove's,
The one only dwelling on earth that she loves.

She looks, and her heart is in heaven: but they fade,
The mist and the river, the hill and the shade;
The stream will not flow, and the hill will not rise,
And the colours have all pass'd away from her eyes!

Byron

The Destruction of Sennacherib

Mentioned by Mark Twain in *Tom Sawyer*, translated into Russian by Tolstoy's cousin Alexei, this version of an Old Testament story has a certain grim charm.

The Assyrian came down like the wolf on the fold,
And his cohorts were gleaming in purple and gold;
And the sheen of their spears was like stars on the sea,
When the blue wave rolls nightly on deep Galilee.

Like the leaves of the forest when Summer is green,
That host with their banners at sunset were seen:
Like the leaves of the forest when Autumn hath blown,
That host on the morrow lay withered and strown.

For the Angel of Death spread his wings on the blast,
And breathed in the face of the foe as he passed;
And the eyes of the sleepers waxed deadly and chill,
And their hearts but once heaved, and for ever
grew still!

And there lay the steed with his nostril all wide,
But through it there rolled not the breath of his pride;
And the foam of his gasping lay white on the turf,
And cold as the spray of the rock-beating surf.

And there lay the rider distorted and pale,
With the dew on his brow, and the rust on his mail:
And the tents were all silent, the banners alone,
The lances unlifted, the trumpet unblown.

And the widows of Ashur are loud in their wail,
And the idols are broke in the temple of Baal;
And the might of the Gentile, unsmote by the sword,
Hath melted like snow in the glance of the Lord.

Now as your poetry-loving editor, I can understand lances unlifted, and I can imagine trumpets unblown, but damned if I can comprehend might unsmote. Another poet, less arcane and more beloved, likewise had a low opinion of this poem:

What does it mean when we are told
That the Assyrian came down like a wolf on the fold?
In the first place, George Gordon Byron had had
  enough experience
To know that it probably wasn't just one Assyrian,
  it was a whole lot of Assyrians.
However, as too many arguments are apt to induce
  apoplexy and thus hinder longevity,
We'll let it pass as one Assyrian for the sake of brevity.
Now then, this particular Assyrian, the one whose
  cohorts were gleaming in purple and gold,

Just what does the poet mean when he says he came
down like a wolf on the fold?
In heaven and earth more than is dreamed of in our
philosophy there are a great many things,
But I don't imagine that among them there is a wolf
with purple and gold cohorts or purple and gold
anythings.
No, no, Lord Byron, before I'll believe that this
Assyrian was actually like a wolf I must have
some kind of proof;
Did he run on all fours and did he have a hairy tail
and a big red mouth and big white teeth and
did he say Woof woof?

~ Ogden Nash, *Very Like a Whale*

Parting Shots

Since Rose Standish died, my life has been weary and dreary.

~ Longfellow, *The Courtship of Miles Standish*

Of physiology from top to toe I sing.

~ Whitman, *One's Self I Sing*

My unwashed Muse pollutes not things divine.

~ Carew, *To My Worthy Friend, G. Sandys*

Your company is as my eyeball dear,
Being far from you, no comfort can be near.

~ Heywood, *A Woman Killed with Kindness*
Act I, Scene 3

The chiming bowels give thanks to their
Maker and broadcast the incense of life lived well.

~ Alan Ansen, *Fatness*

I'll lug the guts into the neighboring room.

~ Shakespeare, *Hamlet,* III, 4.

Dear Sir! if you're in mood to whistle,
As Prologue to my slight Epistle,
I beg your audience for a minute,
In favor of whatever's in it.

~ Boswell, *A Poetical Epistle to Doctor Sterne, Parson Yorick, and Tristram Shandy*

Sweet child of Spring! like thee in sorrow's shade,
Full oft I mourn in tears, and droop forlorn:
And O! like thine, may light my gloom pervade,
And Sorrow fly before Joy's living morn!

~ Ann Radcliffe, *Sonnet, To the Lily*

Words of great pomp, that pleased
The ear of vanity, and made the worms
Of earth mistake themselves for gods.

~ Pollok, *The Course of Time*

My dwelling is the shadow of the night.
Why doth thy magic torture me with light?

~ Byron, *Manfred*

Bonus Elements in the Original Stuffed Owl

Readers who admire epic poems and their neo-classical conventions of antiquated language and solemn addresses to the invisible goddesses of the arts will love the mock epic by co-editor Charles Lee, which begins:

> Bad Verse I sing, and since 'twere best, I deem,
> T'employ a style that suits my swelling theme,
> First, in my lines some flatulence t'infuse,
> I thus invoke the Muddle-headed Muse.

Cartoons that made gentle fun of the literary life were supplied by Max Beerbohm and are replaced in this volume by images acquired gratis online.

Finally, the book's index was a parody of a practical scholarly apparatus that is today less often used since the invention of the Search function. This is a pity, because the traditional form permitted Wyndham Lewis and Lee to compose the most riotously funny index ever devised. Naturally, the conventions of the real index were used—a key word followed by clarification words, in a completely ungrammatical order.

For readers who may not be familiar with this convention, here are some examples:

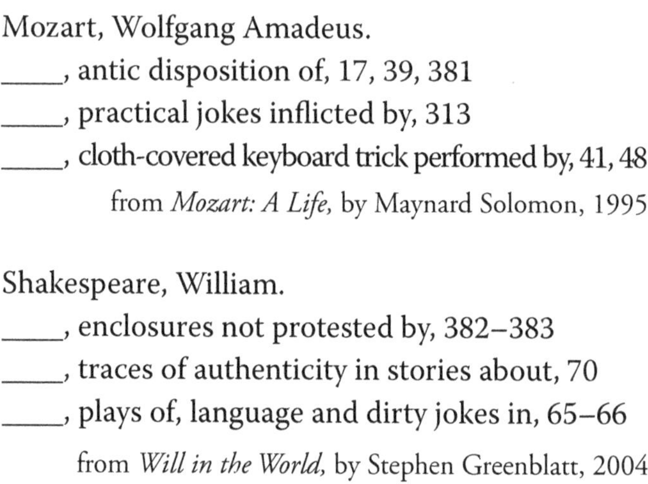

Mozart, Wolfgang Amadeus.
_____, antic disposition of, 17, 39, 381
_____, practical jokes inflicted by, 313
_____, cloth-covered keyboard trick performed by, 41, 48

from *Mozart: A Life,* by Maynard Solomon, 1995

Shakespeare, William.
_____, enclosures not protested by, 382–383
_____, traces of authenticity in stories about, 70
_____, plays of, language and dirty jokes in, 65–66

from *Will in the World,* by Stephen Greenblatt, 2004

The present editor liked *The Stuffed Owl* index so much that she made additions of her own from the same set of verses—or as we say today, from the same database. The reader is urged to secure a copy of the original and to enjoy it for its hundreds of delicious morsels. Furthermore, with your own copy you can find that the following *new* index entries below do, in fact, correctly refer to specific poems in that worthy tome.

Astonishment, causes nations to rush into the tide, 13
Author inadvertently mis-titles his poem, 85–86
Butter, desired for pedicure, 42
Dung-heaps, trodden on by ambitious planters, 91
Deep, The, has horrible wardrobe forced upon it, 13
Drugs, corrosive, recommended to slow swains, 77
Exchange, vast, the whole creation a, 72
Female, polished, 156
Guitar, hoarse, 81
Head, softer than eiderdown, 16
Hatter, beneficiary of sheep's good humor, 77
Horse's mouth, absence of tusks therein, 43
Globe, will probably not disappear, 216
Homicide, enormous, 205
Leeches, decaying, 145
Loan, timely, prevents palsy, 214
Mind, wrecked, outlived by affection, 130
Obsequious service, unable to preserve child, 152
Pigmies, able to pat giants on the back, 210
Peace, thrown about by music and landscapes, 156
Resurrection of the flesh, finds lord and clown in compromising posture, 163
Rank, noble, fatal to village maiden, 244–247
Rose, flits and decomposes, 156
Sandals, mocked by pinions, 127

Stream, implored to stop chasing itself, 34
Teeth, snowy, stealthily corroded by gangrene, 13
Time, expires with mankind, 130; does not outlive the human mind, 130.
Virtues, blooming, 7
Winds, in concert, 73; breathing around, ibid.

Subject Index

The traditional index format has been retained for this collection. Up-to-date readers may wish to devise their own index, emulating the Search function to re-arrange the items, as for this entry given below:

Neighbors > alarmed > hogs > grunting

A

Angels, pallid and wan, 60
Axe, descending, causes condemned men to smile, 56

B

Barb
  dissolves in empty air, 49
  furious, snorts fire and foam, 49
Bed, not a blabber, 86
Bee
  attracted to bosoms, 20, 30
  transmogrifying, 77

Billee (aka Bill, Billy), prepares to recite twelfth commandment, 109
Bouillabaisse, inspires ballad, 62
Bowels
chiming, 123
dissolved by dawn, 100
treated delicately, 6
Brassiere, its resemblance to a poem, 81
Brave, the, dressed by spring with sweet sod, 42
Breast
compared to sheep, 19
source of ambrosial meat, 30
Breath, sweeter than a bean, 19
Buttocks, less delectable, 79

C

Chaste life, conducive to fertility in publication, 17
Constipation, accompanied by whimpering ennui, 2
Cotes, wattled, 68
Cream, unspilled, rises from honey'd sighs, 18
Creatures, scaly, urged to steal from flying lips, 22
Cripple, radiant, 65

D

Daffodil bulbs, found in unexpected place, xi
Dead, the, beautified by time, 52
Disease, vague, spoils the afternoon of rich lady, 61

E

Elf, meddling, 54

F

Face, kiss-worthy, 18
Fingers, cold and dewy, 42
Flesh, putrid, 100

G

Girdle, empty, 79
Glory, trumpet-tongued, 94
Gourd, scooped-out, resembles headgear, 65
Grot, pure, darkened by muddy gloom, 54
Guest, made indecent by phlegm, 92

H

Haps
  not brought in handfuls, 19
  well in spite of itself, 15
Heir of heaven, composed of every possible impulse, 56
Hell, good for frying the soul, 18
Hogs, grunting, alarm the neighbors, 40

I

Infamy, grinning, 41

J

Jones, Mrs., perpetrator of vile deeds, 113

L

Lip, blubber'd, 39
Love
  resembles fart, 33
  resembles feet, 20
  resembles vegetables, 38

M

Maggots, half-formed, 13
Maker, thanked by bowels, 123
Midnight, scared birds of, whizzing round, 48
Muses, implored to help poet heave her verses higher, 102

N

Night-dew, falls and weeps, 51
Noodlers, word, inexplicably shortchanged, 7

O

Ocean, confuses elderly seafarer, 50

P

Pants, cause cream to flow, 18
Piazza, gasping, 79

Q

Queen, wishes she were a flood, 23

R

Reed, oaten, love-sick, 55
Reservoir
- adorned with slime, 80
- good place to bloat, 80

Ring, deposed, 35
Rocks, wild and impending, 44

S

Slime, made of infernal mists, 37
Snail, compendious, 35
Snake, secret, given to shooting stings, 39
Snickersnee, brandished aboard ship, 109
Souls, men's, deflowered by nature and God, 17
Spit, fell, used to defy foe, 37
Spleen, death's, not eager to unlock souls, 64
Stream, hoarse, chides rocks in vain, 107
Subtraction, foul, 78

T

Taffeta, mound of, 81
Toad, speckled, a load of spite and hate, 37
Toilet, thorough but not gay, 97
Trumpet, unblown, 120

U

Ugsome, 13
Universe, explained by poet, 11

V

Verse, bad, unalloyed pleasure in reading, xi–140

Author Index

Alger, Horatio, 71
Ansen, Alan, 123
Arnold, Matthew, 68
Ashbery, John, 80
Boswell, James, 43, 124
Browning, Robert, 63–65, 110–112
Bunner, H. C., 113–115
Byron, George Gordon, Lord, 52, 91, 119–120, 124
Carew, Thomas, 30, 123
Coleridge, Samuel Taylor, 50
Collins, William, 42
Cowper, William, 116–117
Crashaw, Richard, 34
D'Israeli, Isaac, 92
Donne, John, 27
Drayton, Michael, 22
Dryden, John, 39, 88–90
Eliot, Thomas Stearns, 75–76, 100

Finkel, Donald, 81
Fry, Christopher, 93
Gray, Thomas, 41
Greville, Fulke, 17
Herrick, Robert, 28
Heywood, Thomas, 86–87, 123
Hollander, John, 81
Howard, Henry, 16
Hugo, Richard, 80
Jarrell, Randall, 79
Keats, John, 53–54
King, Henry, 29
Layzor, Robert, 79
Lodge, Thomas, 20
Longfellow, Henry Wadsworth, 58, 123
Lovelace, Richard, 35–37
Marlowe, Christopher, 25
Marvell, Andrew, 38
Moore, Thomas, 51
Poe, Edgar Allen, 59–60, 94–96
Pollok, Robert, 55–56, 124
Pope, Alexander, 11, 13, 40
Radcliffe, Ann, 44–46, 106–107, 124
Riley, James Whitcomb, 73
Rostand, Edmond, 97
Scott, Sir Walter, 48
Shakespeare, William, 23–24, 124
Sidney, Mary, Countess of Pembroke, 21, 102–104

Sidney, Sir Philip, 18–19
Suckling, Sir John, 32–33
Tennyson, Alfred Lord, 61
Thackeray, William M., 62, 108–109
Tourneur, Cyril, 85
Whitman, Walt, 6, 66–67, 123
Whittier, John Greenleaf, 57
Wordsworth, William, 47, 118
Wyatt, Thomas, 15

About the Editor

IN THE SPIRIT of full disclosure, it is here announced that this little vessel sets sail on the sea of books under a *nom de plume.* As a lady and a scholar, the editor prefers to keep her academic publications distinct from such frothy *divertissements,* no matter how erudite.

In her present identity, she has perpetrated a novel (a thriller about halting the smuggling of endangered species), short stories (currently in various desk drawers), and a compendium of satirical political limericks composed by herself and three other previously gruntled authors.

Having discovered the original *Stuffed Owl* while at college, she made it her mission to archive as many additional poetic monstrosities as attracted her notice while she was otherwise engaged, and has now accumulated enough material to form a collection and offer it to an eager public.

www.ingramcontent.com/pod-product-compliance
Lightning Source LLC
Chambersburg PA
CBHW061104100726
47911CB00012B/384

* 9 7 8 1 7 3 6 9 8 6 4 1 7 *